PREFACE.

The design of the following little book is to furnish receipts for a select variety of French dishes, explained and described in such a manner as to make them intelligible to American cooks, and practicable with American utensils and American fuel. Those that (according to the original work) cannot be prepared without an unusual and foreign apparatus have been omitted; and also such as can only be accomplished by the consummate skill and long practice of native French cooks.

Many dishes have been left out, as useless in a country where provisions are abundant. On this side of the Atlantic all persons in respectable life can obtain better articles of food than sheeps' tails, calves' ears, &c. and the preparation of these articles (according to the European receipts) is too tedious and complicated to be of any use to the indigent, or to those who can spare but little time for their cookery.

Also, the translator has inserted no receipts which contain nothing different from the usual American mode of preparing the same dishes.

Most of the French Cookery Books introduced into this country have failed in their object, from the evident deficiency of the translators in a competent knowledge of the technical terms of cookery and from the multitude of French words interspersed through the directions, and which cannot, in general, be comprehended without an incessant and troublesome reference to the glossary.

The translator of the following pages has endeavored, according to the best of her ability, to avoid these defects, and has aimed at making a book of practical utility to all those who may have a desire to introduce occasionally at their tables good specimens of the French culinary art.

From these receipts she believes that many advantageous hints may be taken for improvements in American cookery; and she hopes that, upon trial, this little work may be found equally useful in private families, hotels, and boarding-houses.

Philadelphia, September, 1832.

CONSOMMÉ, OR JELLY SOUP.

Into two quarts of cold water, put four pounds of the lean of the best beef-steaks, and a large fowl cut into pieces, four large carrots, four onions, four leeks, a bunch of sweet herbs (parsley, thyme, sweet marjoram, sweet basil, and chives), tied up with a laurel-leaf, or two peach-leaves, and four cloves; add a little salt and pepper. Boil it gently for eight hours, skimming it well; then strain it.

PEASE SOUP.

Take two quarts of dried split peas, the evening before you intend making the soup, and putting them into lukewarm water, let them soak all night. In the morning, put the peas into a pan or pot with three quarts of cold water, a pound of bacon, and a pound of the lean of fresh beef. Cut up two carrots, two onions, and two heads of celery, and put them into the soup, with a bunch of sweet herbs, and three or four cloves. Boil it slowly five or six hours, till the peas can no longer be distinguished, having lost all shape and form; then strain it, and serve it up.

MACCARONI SOUP.

First make some good beef soup (without any vegetables), and when it is sufficiently boiled, strain it through a sieve. Take some maccaroni, in the proportion of half a pound to two quarts of soup. Boil it in water until it is tender, adding to it a little butter. Then lay it on a sieve to drain, and cut it into small pieces. Throw it into the soup, and boil all together ten minutes or more. Grate some rich cheese over it before you send it to table.

CHESTNUT SOUP.

Having made some beef soup without vegetables, strain it, and put in a pint of peeled chestnuts for each quart of soup. Boil it again till the chestnuts have gone all to pieces, and have become a part of the liquid.

A still better way is, to roast or bake the chestnuts first, (having cut a slit in the shell of each,) then peel them, and throw them into the soup ten minutes before you take it from the fire.

ALMOND SOUP.

Take half a pound of shelled sweet almonds, and two ounces of shelled bitter almonds, or peach-kernels. Scald them, to make the skins peel off easily, and when they are blanched, throw them into cold water. Then drain and wipe them dry. Beat them (a few at a time) in a marble mortar, adding as you beat them, a little milk and a little grated lemon-peel.

Have ready two quarts of rich milk, boiled with two sticks of cinnamon and a quarter of a pound of sugar. Stir the almonds gradually into the milk, and let them have one boil up. Prepare some slices of toasted bread, take out a little of the soup and soak them in it. Then lay them in the bottom of a tureen, and pour the soup over them. Grate on some nutmeg.

LOBSTER SOUP.

Having boiled a large lobster, extract all the meat from the shell. Fry in butter some thin slices of bread, put them into a marble mortar, one at a time, alternately with some of the meat of the lobster, and pound the whole to a paste till it is all done. Then melt some butter in a stew-pan, and put in the mixed bread and lobster. Add a quart of boiling milk, with salt, mace, and nutmeg to your taste. Let the whole stew gently for half an hour.

OYSTER SOUP.

Take two quarts of oysters; drain them, and cut out the hard part. Have ready a dozen eggs, boiled hard; cut them in pieces, and pound them in a mortar alternately with the oysters. Boil the liquor of the oysters with a head of celery cut small, two grated nutmegs, a tea-spoonful of mace, and a tea-spoonful of cloves, with two tea-spoonfuls of salt, and a tea-spoonful of whole pepper. When the liquor has boiled, stir in the pounded eggs and oysters, a little at a time. Give it one more boil, and then serve it up.

Salt oysters will not do for soup.

GREEN PEAS SOUP.

Make a good beef soup, with the proportion of four pounds of lean beef to a gallon of water. Boil it slowly, and skim it well. In another pot boil two quarts of green peas, with a large bunch of mint, a little salt, and three or four lumps of loaf sugar. When they are quite soft, take them out, strain them from the water, and mash them in a cullender till all the pulp drips through. Then stir it into the soup after you have taken it up and strained it. Prepare some toasted bread cut into small squares, lay it in a tureen, and pour the soup over it.

When you toast bread for soups, stews, &c. always cut off the crust.

GRAVIES, OR ESSENCES.

BROWN GRAVY. (Jus.)

Put into a sauce-pan, or skillet, five or six onions, and as many carrots cut into small pieces, with about two pounds of scraps of beef, in which there must be none of the fat. Pour over them a pint of water. Cover the pan, and begin with a brisk fire. When the gravy has become brown, add a little boiling water (or broth if you have it), with a tea-spoonful of salt, three or four cloves, and a bunch of sweet herbs. Diminish the fire, and let the gravy stew gently for an hour and a half. Occasionally prick the meat with a fork, and press it with the back of a spoon to extract its juices. Then strain it through a sieve, and let it stand a while before you use it.

In addition to the beef, you may put in pieces of cold goose, or cold duck.

WHITE GRAVY. (Coulis.)

Butter the bottom of a sauce-pan, and put in two pounds of scraps of veal, and, if you have it at hand, some cold fowl, or cold turkey; add two white onions, and four or five blades of mace; pour over it a pint of boiling water, or broth; cover the pan, and set it over a slow fire for five or six hours, pricking and pressing the meat with a fork and spoon. Strain it through a sieve, and if it is too thin, set it again over the fire, to stew a while longer.

ESSENCE OF GAME.

Take scraps of any kind of game (partridges, pheasants, hares, &c.), and also four calves feet, and a few small pieces of ham. Put them all into a stew-pan, with half a bottle of white wine, two carrots, two onions, and a bunch of sweet herbs. Stew them over a slow fire for four hours, and when they are reduced to a jelly, moisten it with four table-spoonfuls of hot water, or broth, stirred in gently. Strain it through a sieve, and then clear it by stirring in the whites of three eggs slightly beaten.

TO CLARIFY GRAVIES, OR ESSENCES

Having strained your gravy through a sieve, beat slightly the whites of three eggs, and stir them into it. Place it again on the fire, and stir it till it comes to a boil; then take it from the fire, and put it away to settle. Strain it then through a napkin, and you will have a transparent jelly excellent for making fine sauces.

VELOUTÉ, OR VELVET ESSENCE.

Take half a pound of scraps of veal, the same quantity of pieces of fowls, and twelve or fifteen mushrooms; stew them slowly in butter, and then add two onions, half a carrot, and a bunch of sweet herbs cut small, three table-spoonfuls of flour, three of boiling water or broth, and salt, pepper, and nutmeg to your taste. Let it stew an hour and a half, and then strain it.

SAUCES, &c.

When sauces are finished with eggs, use only the yolks, and mix them first with but a spoonful or two of the sauce; mix them off the fire. Set on the pan again for two or three moments, but do not let it boil after the eggs are in.

BECHAMEL.

Put into a sauce-pan a quarter of a pound of butter sprinkled with flour, three or four onions, and a carrot cut small, a little parsley, and a dozen mushrooms. Set it over the fire until the butter is melted, and then add three table-spoonfuls of flour stirred into a pint of cream or rich milk, with salt, pepper, and nutmeg to your taste. Stir it till it boils; then reduce the fire, and let the bechamel stew gently for three quarters of an hour. When it is done, strain it, and then stir in the yolks of three eggs.

ANOTHER BECHAMEL.

Cut into dice, or small square pieces, half a pound of bacon or ham, a carrot, a turnip, and two onions. Put them into a sauce-pan, with two large spoonfuls of veal-dripping; add a little butter (about two ounces), and two large spoonfuls of flour. Moisten it with boiling water, or broth. Add nutmeg, cloves, thyme, parsley, salt, and pepper to your taste; also a laurel-leaf. Let it stew for an hour. Strain it, and before you serve it up, squeeze in a little lemon-juice.

DRAWN BUTTER.

Put into a small pan a table-spoonful of flour and a tumbler of water, with salt to your taste, and a little pepper. Stir it till it boils. Then withdraw it from the fire, and add two ounces of butter and a few drops of cold water, with a little lemon-juice, or vinegar. Set it on the stove, or near the fire, and keep it warm till it is wanted.

You may thicken it while boiling with mushrooms, cut small; or after it is done with hard eggs chopped fine, pickled cucumbers chopped, or capers.

MELTED BUTTER—*another way*.

Put into a sauce-pan a quarter of a pound of butter. When quite melted over the fire, throw in a large spoonful of flour, and add a half pint of boiling water, and salt to your taste. Boil it a few minutes, and then put in a tea-spoonful of cold water. If intended as sauce for a pudding, stir in at the last a glass of white wine, and half a grated nutmeg.

COLD SAUCE FOR FISH.

Cut small, and pound in a mortar, equal proportions of parsley, chervil, tarragon, chives and burnet, with two yolks of hard-boiled eggs. Pass these ingredients through a cullender, and then mix them on a plate with four table-spoonfuls of sweet oil, two of vinegar, and two of mustard. Use a wooden spoon.

SAUCE FOR VEGETABLES—SUCH AS ASPARAGUS, &c.

Take the yolks of three hard-boiled eggs; mash them on a plate with the back of a wooden spoon, and mix them with three table-spoonfuls of vinegar, a shalot or small onion minced fine, and a little salt and Cayenne pepper. Add three table-spoonfuls of olive oil, and mix the whole very well.

PUNGENT SAUCE. (SAUCE PIQUANTE.)

Put into a saucepan a half-pint of vinegar, a branch of thyme, two or three sprigs of sweet marjoram, a leaf of laurel, a clove of garlic, a shalot or a little onion, and Cayenne pepper and salt to your taste. Add a glass of broth or gravy. Stew the whole slowly till it is reduced to two thirds of the original quantity: then strain it.

ANCHOVY SAUCE—FOR FISH.

Cut the flesh of three anchovies into small shreds, and steep them in vinegar for half an hour or more. Then mince them fine, and throw them into a saucepan with a little butter rolled in flour. Add pepper and mustard to your taste. Pour in sufficient vinegar to cover it, and let it boil gently for a quarter of an hour. Strain it, and squeeze in a little lemon-juice before you serve it up.

CURRY SAUCE.

Put into a sauce-pan two ounces of butter and a table-spoonful of curry-powder (or of powdered turmeric if more convenient), half a grated nutmeg, half a spoonful of saffron, and two spoonfuls of flour. Add sufficient boiling water or broth to cover it, and let it stew a quarter of an hour. Strain it, stir in a little more butter, and serve it up.

TOMATA SAUCE.

Bake ten tomatas, with pepper and salt, till they become like a marmalade. Then add a little flour or grated bread crumbs, and a little broth or hot water. Stew it gently ten minutes, and before you send it to table add two ounces of butter and let it melt in the sauce.

CUCUMBER SAUCE.

Put into a sauce-pan a piece of butter rolled in flour, some salt, pepper, and one or two pickled cucumbers minced fine. Moisten it with boiling water. Let it stew gently a few minutes, and serve it up.

BREAD SAUCE.

Take four ounces of grated stale bread; pour over it sufficient milk to cover it, and let it soak about three quarters of an hour, or till it becomes incorporated with the milk. Then add a dozen corns of black pepper, a little salt, and a piece of butter the size of a walnut. Pour on a little more milk, and give it a boil. Serve it up in a sauce-boat, and eat it with roast wild fowl, or roast pig.

Instead of the pepper, you may boil in it a hand full of dried currants, well picked, washed, and floured.

SAUCE ROBERT.

Put into a sauce-pan a quarter of a pound of butter, with a spoonful of flour. Simmer them till of a fine brown color. Mince half a dozen large onions, and a large slice of cold ham. Put them into the pan, with another piece of butter, and a very little broth or warm water. Skim the sauce well, and let it stew gently for twenty minutes. Before you serve it up,stir in a table-spoonful of lemon-juice or vinegar, and a tea-spoonful of mustard. This sauce is used chiefly for fresh pork, or white poultry.

SHALOT OR ONION SAUCE. (Sauce Ravigote.)

Take a handful of sweet herbs and the same quantity of shalots or little onions, and cut them up small. Put them into a sauce-pan, with some vinegar, salt, pepper, and sufficient broth or warm water to cover them. Let them boil gently for a quarter of an hour. Take the sauce from the fire and set it on the stove, or on the hearth, and stir in (till it melts) a piece of butter rolled in flour, or a spoonful of olive oil.

UNIVERSAL SAUCE.

Take a pint of good broth, or a pint of drawn butter. Stir into it a glass of white wine, and half the peel of a lemon grated. Add a laurel leaf, or two or three peach-leaves, and a spoonful of vinegar. Let the mixture simmer on a few coals or on hot ashes, for five or six hours or more, and it will be good to pour over either meat, poultry, or fish, and will keep several days in a cool place.

LOBSTER SAUCE.

The lobster being boiled, extract the meat from the shell, and beat it in a mortar. Rub it through a cullender or sieve, and put it into a sauce-pan with a spoonful of velouté (or velvet essence) if you have it, and one of broth. Mix it well, and add a piece of butter, some salt, and some Cayenne pepper. Stew it ten minutes, and serve it up, to eat with boiled fresh fish.

SPINACH FOR COLORING GREEN.

Take three handfuls of spinach, and pound it in a mortar to extract the juice. Then put it into a sauce-pan and set it over a slow fire. When it is just ready to boil, take it off and strain it. By stirring in a small quantity of spinach-juice, you may give any sauce a green color.

GARLIC BUTTER.

Take two large cloves of garlic and pound them to a paste in a mortar, adding, by degrees, a piece of butter the size of an egg. You may with a little of this butter give the taste of garlic to sauces. Some persons like a piece of garlic butter on the table, to eat with roast meat.

HAZELNUT BUTTER.

Having scalded and blanched some hazelnuts, pound them to a paste in a mortar, adding gradually a small quantity of butter.

This is good to eat with wild fowl, or to flavor the most delicate sauces.

LARDING.

Larding with slips of fat bacon greatly improves the taste and appearance of meat, poultry, game, &c. and is much used in French cookery.

For this purpose, you must have a larding-pin (which may be purchased at the hardware stores); it is a steel instrument about a foot in length, sharp at one end, and cleft at the other into four divisions which are near two inches long, and resembling tweezers.

Bacon is the proper meat to lard with; the fat only is used. Cut it into slips not exceeding two inches in length, half an inch in breadth, and half an inch in thickness, and smaller if intended for poultry; they will diminish in cooking. Put these slips of bacon (one at a time) into the cleft or split end of the larding-pin. Give each slip a slight twist and press it down hard into the pin, with your fingers. Then run the pin through the meat or fowl (avoiding the bones), and when you draw it out on the under side it will have left the slip of bacon sticking in the upper side. Take care to arrange the slips in regular rows and at equal distances; have them all of the same size, and let every one stick up about an inch from the surface of the meat. If any are wrong, take them out and do them over again.

Fowls and birds are generally larded on the breast only. To lard handsomely and neatly, practice and dexterity are requisite.

Cold poultry may be larded with slips of the fat of cold boiled ham, and when not to be cooked again, it may be made to look very tastefully.

The slips for cold poultry should be very small, scarcely thicker than a straw.

PART THE SECOND.

MEATS.

VEAL À LA MODE.

Rub a fillet of veal all over with salt, and then lard it. Make a seasoning of chopped sweet-herbs, shalots, mushrooms, pepper, salt, and powdered nutmeg, and mace. Moisten it with sweet oil, and cover the veal all over with it. Put the veal into a tureen, and let it set for several hours or all night. Then take it out, covered as it is with the seasoning, and wrap it in two sheets of white paper, well buttered, and roast or bake it. When it is quite done, take off the paper, and scrape off all the seasoning from the veal. Put the seasoning into a sauce-pan with the gravy, the juice of half a lemon, a piece of butter rolled in flour, and a little salt. Give it a boil, skim it well, and pour it over the veal.

VEAL CUTLETS.

Make a seasoning of grated bread, minced ham, chopped parsley, salt, pepper, and chopped mushrooms if you have them. Mix with it some yolk of egg. Cut the veal into small thin slices, rub them all over with lard, and then spread the seasoning over both sides. Wrap up each cutlet carefully in white paper, oiled or buttered. Bake them slowly for three quarters of an hour, and serve them up in the papers.

BLANQUETTE OR FRICASSEE OF VEAL.

Take the remains of a cold roast fillet, or loin of veal. Cut it into small thin pieces. Put them into a stew-pan with a piece of butter rolled in flour, salt, pepper, a few small onions minced, a bunch of sweet-herbs chopped, and one or two laurel or peach-leaves. Mix all together. Pour in a little warm water, and let it boil gently five minutes or more. When you take it off, stir in some lemon-juice and some yolk of egg slightly beaten.

GODIVEAU.

Take a large piece of fillet of veal, free from fat or skin. Mince it small, and then pound it in a mortar till it is a smooth paste. Afterwards rub it through a cullender or sieve.

Soak some slices of bread in warm milk, and rub the bread also through a sieve. There must be an equal quantity of bread and veal. Take the same proportion of butter, and beat it in a mortar with pepper, salt, nutmeg, and chopped parsley to your taste. Then put all together. Beat two or three eggs till very light, and add them gradually to the mixture. Make it into round balls or into long rolls, and fry them in butter. Or you may put it into a pie (without a lid) and bake it.

Godiveau is a very fine stuffing for poultry or wild fowl.

CALVES' LIVER BAKED.

Lard the liver with bacon, and let it lie three or four hours in a covered tureen with a seasoning of parsley, shalots, laurel and thyme chopped small, a little pepper and salt, and two table-spoonfuls of sweet oil. Turn it several times. Then wrap it up in thin slices of bacon or cold ham, and bake or roast it about an hour and a quarter. Add to the gravy the yolk of an egg, and some minced onions and chopped sweet-herbs.

CALVES' LIVER FRIED.

Cut the liver into thin slices, and put them into a frying-pan with a piece of butter rolled in flour, some minced onions and a glass of white wine, salt, pepper, and a little mace. Let it fry about ten minutes.

VEAL KIDNEYS.

Cut the kidneys into thin slices; having first soaked them in cold water, rub them with a little salt and pepper. Then sprinkle them with flour, and a little parsley and onions minced fine. Fry them in butter, adding a glass of champagne or other white wine.

Mutton kidneys may be done in the same manner.

Another way of dressing kidneys is to split them in half, season them with salt and pepper, lard them, and broil them.

GRILLADES.

Cut slices from either a fillet of veal, a round of fresh beef, a leg of mutton, or a leg of pork. Do not let them exceed the thickness of half an inch. Put them into a stew-pan with a sufficient proportion of oil, pepper, salt, and a little parsley and onion chopped fine. Stew them in a very little water till half done. Then prepare some sheets of white paper rubbed with oil or butter. Take out the slices of meat (covered with this seasoning) and grate some bread crumbs over them. Fasten up each slice in a piece of paper, and broil them on a gridiron over a slow fire. Serve them up in the paper.

LIVER CAKE.

Take a pound and a half of grated bread, and two pounds of liver (either calves' or pigs') a few onions, a little sage, some mushrooms, and a laurel leaf, all chopped fine. Mince the liver also, and mix it with the other ingredients, adding salt, pepper, and nutmeg. Butter a mould or a very deep dish. Put the mixture into it, and let it bake an hour and a half in a moderate oven. When done, turn it out.

It is eaten cold, cut in slices.

SIRLOIN OF BEEF.

Rub your beef all over with salt, and lard the lean part of it with slips of fat bacon. Cover the meat with sheets of oiled or buttered paper. Roast it in proportion to its size, between three and four hours.

Serve it up with its gravy, and have some onion sauce in a boat.

STEWED BEEF.

Take some slices of cold roast beef that has been under-done. Put them into a stew-pan with a little gravy or broth, or if you have neither, some warm water. Add a piece of butter rolled in flour, some capers, or some pickled cucumbers chopped small, a little lemon-juice or vinegar, and some salt and pepper. Let the beef simmer slowly, but do not allow it to boil. Have ready some slices of bread (of the same size as the slices of beef) and fry them in butter. Put some tomata sauce in the bottom of a dish. Lay on it in a pile a few slices of beef and slices of fried bread alternately. Pour the gravy over it, and send it to table.

Any other sort of meat may be done in the same manner.

BEEF STEAKS.

Cut slices of beef from the sirloin. Trim them neatly, and take off the bone and the skin. To make them tender beat them on both sides with a wooden beetle or with the end of a rolling-pin. Rub them with salt and pepper. Warm a sufficient quantity of butter, and when it is soft spread it over the steaks. Then sprinkle them with onions minced very fine. Cover them up in a dish, and let them lie an hour or more in the seasoning. Then broil them over a clear fire. Slice some cold boiled potatoes, fry them in butter, and lay them round the steaks.

BEEF À LA MODE.

Take a round of fresh beef, and beat it well to make it tender. Rub it all over with salt and pepper. Lard it on both sides with slips of bacon. Lay it in a deep pan with some slices of bacon, a calves-foot, a few onions, a carrot cut in pieces, a bunch of sweet herbs cut small, one or two laurel leaves, some cloves, and a beaten nutmeg. Pour in a half-pint of red wine, a half-pint of white wine, and a spoonful of brandy. Let it stew slowly for at least six hours. Then take it out; strain the gravy, pour it over the meat, and serve it up.

A fillet of veal may be done in the same manner.

ROASTED HAM.

Let your ham soak all night in cold water, and then trim it handsomely, having first taken out the bone by loosening the meat all round it, with the point of a knife. Tie a broad tape round the ham to keep it in shape. Then put it into a large pan with some sliced onions, some sprigs of parsley, two or three laurel leaves, and a bottle of white wine. Cover it, and let it lie in the seasoning twenty-four hours. Then roast it, and baste it with the seasoning. A large ham will require four or five hours to roast. A little before it is done, take off the skin and sprinkle the ham with grated bread crumbs.

While the ham is roasting, stew together the bone and the trimmings and scraps till they come to a jelly, which you must strain through a sieve. When you take the ham from the spit (having removed the tape that has been fastened round it) glaze it all over with the jelly, laid on with a brush or a quill feather. Serve it up with the seasoning or marinade under it.

If the ham is to be eaten cold, you may cover it all over the glazing with cold boiled potatoes grated finely, so that it will look like a large cake covered with icing. Ornament it with slices of boiled carrot, beets, &c. scolloped and laid on the potatoes, in handsome forms, so as to look like red and yellow flowering. Stick a large bunch of double parsley in the centre.

A ham boiled in the usual manner may be ornamented in the same way; first extracting the bone, and making the meat into a circular shape.

Instead of a mere bunch of double parsley, you may stick in the centre of the ham a nosegay of flowers, formed of different culinary vegetables, and cut into proper shape with a sharp pen-knife. All these vegetables must be raw. The flowers intended to represent red roses must be made of beets, the white roses of turnips, and the marigolds or other deep yellow flowers must be cut out of carrots. The pieces of turnips and beets must first be made with the pen-knife into the form of a ball, on the surface of which the rose-leaves must be cut. The carrots may be cut into flat slices, and then notched to look like marigolds or chrysanthemums. Stick each flower on the end of a small wooden skewer, which will answer for the stalk, but which must be concealed by thick bunches of double parsley tied on so as to represent the green leaves. Tie all the skewers together at the bottom with a pack-thread, and the whole will have the effect of a handsome nosegay when placed in the middle of the ham.

A round of cold à-la-mode beef may be ornamented with a bunch of these flowers. Let the beef itself be covered all over with parsley, so as to resemble a green bank.

FRIED HAM, WITH TOMATAS.

Fry some slices of cold boiled ham. Then fry some tomatas, allowing one tomata to each slice of meat. Lay the tomatas on the ham, shake some pepper over them, and send them to table.

ROASTED TONGUE.

Having soaked a large smoked tongue all night in cold water, parboil it in a very little warm water with a slice of bacon, a bunch of sweet herbs, and an onion or two stuck with cloves. When it is nearly done, take it out, drain it, and lard it with large slips of bacon on the upper side, and small pieces on the under side. Then put it on the spit and roast it half an hour, and serve it up with pungent sauce (Sauce Piquante.)

BAKED TONGUE.

Take a cold boiled tongue and cut it into slices. Put in the bottom of a deep dish a little vinegar, with some capers, parsley and shalots minced fine, and some grated bread, all mixed together. Lay the slices of tongue upon this, and cover them with some more of the same seasoning. Then grate some bread all over the top. Moisten the whole by pouring in a little warm water. Put the dish into a stove moderately heated, or set it on a slow furnace. Bake it till brown.

POTTED TONGUE.

Boil two smoked tongues. Skin them and cut them into thin slices. Put the slices (a few at a time) into a mortar and beat them to a paste, adding gradually a pound of butter. Then prepare an equal quantity of the lean of stewed veal, and pound that also in the mortar (a little at a time) with the same proportion of butter. Then make the veal and the tongue into lumps, and put them alternately into your stone pots, pressing them together so as to look like red and white marble. Have a layer of veal at the top. Press the whole down very hard. Fill up the pots with butter, boiled and skimmed and poured on warm. Tie them up closely with parchment, and keep them in a cold but dry place.

When you use it, cut it in slices.

LEG OF MUTTON WITH OYSTERS.

Rub a leg of mutton all over with salt, and put it on the spit to roast with a clear fire, basting it with its own gravy. When it is nearly done, take it up and with a sharp knife make incisions all over it, and stuff an oyster into every hole. Then put it again before the fire, to finish roasting.

Before you serve it up, skim the gravy well, and give it a boil with a glass of red wine.

CUTLETS À LA MAINTENON.

Cut a neck of mutton into chops, leaving a bone to each, but scraping the end of the bone quite clean. Mix together some grated bread, and some marjoram and onion chopped fine. Season it with pepper, salt, and nutmeg. Having melted some butter, dip each chop into it, and then cover them on both sides with the seasoning. Butter some half-sheets of white paper, and put the cutlets into them, leaving the end of each bone to stick out of the paper like a handle. Lay them on a gridiron, and broil them for about twenty minutes on clear lively coals. Serve them up in the papers.

Make a sauce of four shalots or little onions chopped fine, some gravy, a little pepper and salt, and a spoonful of red wine. Boil this sauce for a minute, and send it up in a boat.

PORK CUTLETS.

Mince together some onions, parsley, and a laurel leaf. Season it with pepper, salt, and cloves. Cut your pork into thin steaks, and lay them in this seasoning for five or six hours. Then broil or fry them with the seasoning on them, and serve them up with sauce Robert, or with tomata sauce.

LARDED RABBIT.

Lard a fine large rabbit, and put it into a stew-pan with a slice or two of cold ham, a bunch of sweet-herbs, a table-spoonful of sweet oil, and a gill of white wine. Stew it slowly, and, when it is quite done, strain the gravy and pour it over the rabbit.

RABBITS IN PAPERS.

Take two young rabbits; cut off the limbs and put them aside. Cut the flesh from the body, and chop it very fine, mixing it with shalots, parsley, and mushrooms chopped also, and, if you choose, a clove of garlic. Season it with salt, pepper, and nutmeg, and moisten it with sweet oil. Lay the legs of the rabbit in this mixture, for three or four hours. Then take out separately each leg covered with the seasoning, lay on it a thin slice of bacon or cold ham, and wrap it in a sheet of white paper well buttered. Broil the limbs slowly on the gridiron, and serve them up hot in the papers.

Fowls may be done in the same manner. Ducks also.

PILAU.

Take half a dozen slices of the lean of a leg of mutton, or of fillet of veal. Put them into a stew-pan with six large onions, a carrot cut in pieces, and some parsley, with pepper, salt, and nutmeg to your taste. Add a tea-spoonful of saffron, a piece of butter rolled in flour, and a little boiling water. Let it stew for an hour, and skim it well.

Have ready a pound of rice boiled soft and drained. Mix with it a large piece of butter. Put some rice in the bottom of a deep dish, and lay on it first the seasoning, and then the slices of meat in a pile. Keep the remainder of the rice over it, and set it on the stove or in the oven for ten minutes.

VEAL SWEETBREADS.

Take three sweet-breads, and soak them three or four hours in milk. Then wipe them dry, and lard them. Make a seasoning of sweet-herbs and mushrooms chopped fine, a quarter of a pound of cold ham or bacon scraped or minced, salt, pepper, and nutmeg to your taste, and a tablespoonful of sweet-oil. Mix the seasoning very well together, and put it into a stew-pan with the sweet-breads, a piece of butter rolled in flour, a little water or broth, and the same quantity of wine. Stew it about ten minutes. Then take out the sweet-breads, lay them in a deep dish, pour the seasoning over them, and let them get cold. Next prepare some cases of white paper, oil them, and cover the inside with grated bread. Put a sweet-bread into each paper-case, with some of the seasoning at bottom and top. Close the cases, put them in an oven, and bake them long enough to color the sweet-breads. Serve them up in the papers.

Set the gravy over the fire, and when it simmers take it off, and stir in the yolk of an egg slightly beaten. Keep it covered for a few minutes, and then serve it up in a boat.

PART THE THIRD.

GAME AND POULTRY.

A SALMI.

Cut off the flesh from the bodies of a pair of cold pheasants, partridges or wild-ducks, or an equal quantity of small birds. Beat it in a mortar, moistening it frequently with a little broth or gravy. Then pass the whole through a cullender or sieve. Put it into a stew-pan with a piece of butter about the size of a walnut, rolled in flour; half a pint of port wine or claret; two whole onions, and a bunch of sweet-herbs. Let it boil half an hour, and then stir in two table-spoonfuls of sweet oil, and the juice of a lemon.

In another pan stew the legs and wings of the birds, but do not let them boil. Stew them in butter rolled in flour, seasoned with pepper and salt. Cut some slices of bread into triangular pieces, and fry them in butter. Lay them in the bottom of a dish, put the legs and wings upon them, and then the other part of the stew. Garnish the edge with slices of lemon, handsomely notched with a knife.

If the Salmi is made of partridges, use oranges instead of lemons for the juice and garnishing.

COLD SALMI.

This is prepared on the table. Take the liver of a roast goose, turkey, or ducks. Put some of the gravy on a plate, cut up the liver in it, and bruise it with the back of a spoon or a silver fork. Add three tea-spoonfuls of olive oil, the juice of a lemon, and cayenne pepper and salt to your taste. Mix it well. When the bird is cut up, eat with it some of this sauce.

RAGOOED LIVERS.

Take the livers of half a dozen fowls or other poultry, a dozen mushrooms, a bunch of sweet herbs, a clove of garlic or a small onion, a table-spoonful of butter rolled in flour. Add a glass of white wine, and sufficient warm water to keep the ingredients moist. Season it with salt and pepper. Stew all together, and skim it well. Before you send it to table, stir in the yolks of two or three beaten eggs, and two spoonfuls of cream.

A FINE HASH.

Take any cold game or poultry that you have. You may mix several kinds together. Some sausages, of the best sort, will be an improvement. Chop all together, and mix with it bread crumbs, chopped onions and parsley, and the yolks of two or three hard-boiled eggs. Put it into a sauce-pan with a proportionate piece of butter rolled in flour. Moisten it with broth, gravy, or warm water, and let it stew gently for half an hour.

Cold veal or fresh pork may be hashed in the same manner.

MARINADE OF FOWLS.

Take a pair of fowls, skin and cut them up. Wash them in lukewarm water. Drain them, and put them into a stew-pan with some butter. Season them to your taste with salt, pepper, and lemon-juice. Add parsley, onions, and a laurel leaf. Moisten them with warm water, and let them stew slowly on hot coals for two or three hours. Clear them from the seasoning and drain them. Then lay them in a dish, and grate bread crumbs over them. Whip some white of egg to a stiff froth, and cover with it all the pieces of fowl.

FRICASSEE OF FOWLS.

Skin and cut up your fowls, and soak them two hours in cold water, to make them white. Drain them. Put into a stew-pan a large piece of butter, and a table-spoonful of flour. Stir them together till the butter has melted. Add salt, pepper, a grated nutmeg, and a bunch of sweet-herbs. Pour in half a pint of cream. Put in the fowls, and let them stew three quarters of an hour. Before you send them to table, stir in the yolks of three beaten eggs, and the juice of half a lemon.

The Fricassee will be greatly improved by some mushrooms stewed with the fowl.

To keep the fricassee white, cover it (while stewing) with a sheet of buttered paper laid over the fowls. The lid of the stew-pan must be kept on tightly.

FOWLS WITH TARRAGON.

Pick two handfuls of tarragon (the leaves from the stalks) and chop half of it fine with the livers of the fowls. Mix it with butter, salt, and whole pepper. Stuff your fowls with it. Lard them and wrap them in papers buttered or oiled.

Melt some butter rolled in flour, and stir into it the rest of the tarragon. Moisten it with a little water or milk. Stir in the yolks of two beaten eggs, and the juice of half a lemon. Serve it up as gravy. Strew over the fowls some sprigs of fresh tarragon.

A STEWED FOWL.

Take a large fowl, and put it into a stew-pan with two ounces or more of butter, some thin slices of cold ham, a little parsley and onion chopped fine, and some nutmeg, salt, and pepper. Then pour in half a tumbler of white wine. You may add, if you choose, six table-spoonfuls of boiled rice, which you must afterwards serve up under the fowl and ham. Let it stew slowly for two hours, with just sufficient water to keep it from burning.

Before you send it to table, go all over the fowl with a feather or brush dipped in yolk of egg. You may add to the stew a dozen small onions, to be laid round the fowl with the slices of ham.

CHICKENS IN JELLY.

Cold chickens, pigeons, and game, look very handsome in jelly. To make this jelly, take four calves-feet (with the skin on) and boil them to a strong jelly with an ounce of isinglass and three quarts of water, carefully skimming off the fat. The calves-feet must be boiled the day before the jelly is wanted, and when it is cold scrape off all the sediment that adheres to it. Then boil the jelly with the addition of the whites and shells of six eggs, the juice of three lemons, three or four sticks of cinnamon, half a pound of loaf-sugar, and a pint of Malaga or other sweet wine. Let it boil hard for five or six minutes, but do not stir it. Strain it several times through a flannel bag into a deep white pan, but do not on any consideration squeeze or press the bag, as that will entirely spoil the transparency of the jelly. After it has done dripping through the bag, take out all the ingredients (as they are now of no farther use) and wash the bag clean. Then pour the jelly into it again, and let it strain. Repeat this till it is perfectly clear and bright; washing the bag every time. Sometimes (but not often) it will be clear at the first straining.

Put a little of the jelly into the bottom of a deep dish or bowl, and set it in a cold place. When it has congealed and is firm, lay your chickens on it with the breasts downwards. Having kept the remainder of the jelly warm, to prevent its congealing too soon, pour it over the fowls. Let it stand all night or till it is perfectly firm. Then set your dish or bowl in warm water for a moment, to loosen the jelly. Lay over it the dish in which you intend to serve it up, and turn it out carefully. If you fear that you will not be able to turn it out without breaking the jelly, you may prepare it at the beginning in a deep china dish fit to send to table.

If you put too much water to the calves-feet, the jelly will never be firm, till it is boiled over again with more isinglass. The generality of cooks are in the habit of putting too much water to every thing, and should be cautioned accordingly.

PULLED CHICKENS.

Boil a pair of fowls till they are about half done. Then skin them, and pull the flesh from the bones in pieces about a finger in breadth and half a finger in length. Take a few table-spoonfuls of the liquor they were boiled in, and mix it with half a pint of boiling cream. Put it into a stew-pan with a piece of butter rolled in flour; pepper, salt, and nutmeg; a little chopped parsley; and a table-spoonful of white wine. Put in the pieces of chicken, and stew them slowly till quite done.

STEWED TURKEY, OR TURKEY EN DAUBE.

Take a large turkey; lard it and stuff it as for roasting. Then cover it all over with a seasoning made of salt, pepper, nutmeg, and sweet-herbs, parsley and onions, minced fine. Put it into a stew-pan, with some slices of bacon, one or two calves-feet, some onions and carrots, one or two laurel leaves, a few cloves, a beaten nutmeg, salt, pepper, and, if you choose, a clove of garlic. Pour in a pint of water, and a pint of white wine or brandy.

Put on the cover of the stew-pan, and lay round its edge on the outside a wet cloth, which must be kept wet. Stew it slowly for five or six hours or more, and turn the turkey when about half done. When it is finished, withdraw the fire, and skim and strain the gravy. Serve up the turkey with the gravy under it.

A goose done this way is very fine.

A round of beef may be stewed in the same manner. It will be the better for lying all night in the seasoning, and it should be put in to stew early in the morning.

ROASTED TURKEY.

Rub the turkey all over with salt. Then lard it. You may stuff it with sausage-meat; or with chestnuts previously boiled, peeled, and mashed. Or, you may make a force-meat stuffing of the liver, heart, and gizzard, chopped fine, and mixed with chopped parsley, onions, sweet-herbs, grated bread, butter, lemon-juice, grated lemon-peel, and the yolk of one or two eggs.

A turkey of moderate size will require at least two hours to roast. Thicken the gravy with yolk of egg stirred in just before you send it to table.

A cold roast turkey should be larded and served up with large spoonfuls of stiff currant jelly dropped all over it.

You may roast a goose in the same manner.

POTTED GOOSE.

Take several fine geese; rub them with salt, and put into each a handful of sage leaves. Roast them about an hour. Do not baste them, but save all the fat in the dripping-pan, emptying it as it is filled. When you have taken the geese from the spit, cut off the legs and wings, and cut the flesh from the breast in slices. Set them away to get cold.

Put the fat that has dripped from the geese into a kettle, with about half as much lard as there is of the dripping. Boil it ten minutes. Have ready a tall stone jar, or more than one if necessary. Lay two legs of the geese side by side in the bottom, and sprinkle them with salt and pepper; placing, if you choose, a laurel leaf on each. Then put in two wings, and season them also. Next a layer of the slices cut from the breast, seasoned in the same manner. When the pots are almost full of the goose, fill them up to the top with the boiling fat, and set them away till the next day to get cold. The upper layer must be covered at least an inch thick with the fat.

Tie up the pots with covers of parchment wet with brandy, and keep them in a cold but not in a damp place.

In France great numbers of geese are fattened for this purpose.

DUCKS WITH TURNIPS.

Stew some turnips with butter, salt, and a little sugar. When soft, take them out and drain them. Cut up your ducks, season them, and put them into the same pan that has held the turnips. Stew the ducks with a piece of butter rolled in flour, a little water, and a bunch of sweet-herbs tied up. When the ducks are nearly done, put the turnips in again, and let all stew slowly together for ten minutes, skimming it well. Withdraw the sweet-herbs before you send the dish to table.

A DUCK WITH OLIVES.

Having larded your duck, stew it whole, with butter, pepper, salt, and a little water. Take half a pint of olives, cut them in half and take out the seeds or stones. When the duck is nearly done, throw in the olives, and let all stew together about five minutes or more. Serve up the duck with the olives round it.

A DUCK WITH PEAS.

Stew the duck whole, with some lard and a little salt, till about half done. Then take it out and drain it. Put into the stew-pan a large piece of butter rolled in flour. When it has melted, pour in a quart of shelled green peas, and add a bunch of mint, or other sweet herbs, and some pepper and salt. Then put in the duck, adding a little warm water. Let it stew slowly till quite done, skimming it well.

TURKEY PUDDINGS.

Mince thirty small onions and mix them with an equal quantity of bread crumbs that have been soaked in milk. Chop an equal quantity of the flesh of cold turkey. Mix all together, and pound it very well in a mortar. Pass it through a cullender, and then return it to the mortar and beat it again, adding gradually the yolks of six hard eggs, and a pint of cream or half a pound of butter. Season it to your taste with salt, mace and nutmeg.

Have ready some skins, nicely cleaned as for sausages. Fill the skins with the mixture, and tie up the ends. Then simmer your puddings, but do not let them boil. Take them out, drain them, and put them away to get cold.

When you wish to cook them for immediate use prick them with a fork, wrap them in buttered paper, and broil them on a gridiron.

Similar puddings may be made of cold fowls.

BAKED PIGEONS, OR PIGEONS À LA CRAPAUDINE.

Split the pigeons down the back. Take out the livers, which you must mince with bacon and sweet-herbs, adding to them the livers of fowls or other birds, if you have them, and bacon in proportion. Or you may substitute sausage-meat. Add bread-crumbs soaked in milk, and the yolks of two eggs or more, with salt, pepper, mace and nutmeg to your taste. Mix all together, and stuff your pigeons with it, and then glaze them all over with beaten white of egg. Place them in a buttered pan, and set them in the oven. Bake them half an hour. Before you serve them up, squeeze some lemon-juice into the gravy.

BROILED PIGEONS.

Split your pigeons and flatten them. Make a seasoning of sweet oil, salt, pepper, chopped shalots, and chopped parsley. Rub this seasoning all over the pigeons. Then cover them with grated bread crumbs. Wrap each in a sheet of white paper, and broil them on a slow fire. Serve them up with a sauce made of minced onions, butter rolled in flour, lemon-juice or vinegar, and salt and pepper.

PIGEONS PEAR-FASHION. (PIGEONS AU POIRE.)

First, bone your pigeons. To do this, take a sharp knife, and slipping it under the flesh carefully loosen it from the bone, and do not tear the skin. Begin at the upper part of the bird, just above the wings, scrape gradually down, and finish at the legs. Then take hold of the neck, and draw out the whole skeleton at once. Make a good force-meat or stuffing (as directed for baked pigeons), and fill them with it, making them each into the shape of a large pear. Fasten them with skewers. Glaze them all over with yolk of egg, and then roll them in grated bread-crumbs. Stick in the top of each, the lower end of the leg, to look like the stem of a pear. Lay them in a buttered dish (but not so close as to touch each other) and bake them. Make a good gravy, thickened with the yolk of an egg, and some butter rolled in flour.

PIGEONS WITH PEAS.

Take two or four pigeons (according to their size), and truss them with the feet inwards. Put them into a stew-pan with a piece of butter rolled in flour, and two or three slices of cold ham, or bacon, and a little water. Let them stew gently till brown. Then add a quart of green peas, and a bunch of mint, with another piece of butter, and a little warm water or milk. Let them stew slowly, and when they are quite done, stir in some more butter. Serve up the pigeons with the peas under them.

ROASTED PARTRIDGES.

Lard the partridges, and put in the inside of each a laurel leaf, and an orange cut in pieces. If you omit the laurel leaf, do not peel the orange, but put in the pieces with the rind on them. These must be taken out before the partridges are sent to table. Be careful not to roast them too much.

PARTRIDGES WITH CABBAGE.

Having trussed the partridges, put them into a stew-pan with a large piece of butter rolled in flour; a quarter of a pound of bacon or ham cut into dice; a bunch of sweet-herbs, and a little warm water. Put into another stew-pan a fine Savoy cabbage, with a pint of the dripping of beef or pork. Let it stew slowly till nearly done. Then take out the cabbage and drain it, and put it into the stew-pan to cook with the partridges for half an hour. Lay the cabbage under the partridges when you send them to table.

A PARTRIDGE PIE.

Take three pair of large partridges and truss them as you do fowls. Rub them all over with a mixture of pepper, salt, powdered mace and powdered nutmeg. Take a pound of fat bacon and two pounds of lean veal, and cut them into small pieces. Put them into a stew-pan with a quarter of a pound of butter. Add a bunch of sweet-herbs, and a few shalots or small onions, all minced fine. Stew them till the meat seems to be quite done, and then put it into a cullender to drain. Afterwards put the meat into a mortar, season it with pepper, salt, nutmeg and mace, and pound it to a smooth paste; moistening it at times with some of the liquor in which it was stewed.

Prepare a rich paste, and spread a sheet of it over the bottom of a large and deep buttered dish. Put in the partridges, side by side, pour in a little water, add a piece of butter, and cover them with the pounded meat. Lay on the top a few slices of cold ham. Roll out a thick piece of paste for the lid, and cover the pie with it; cutting the edges into square notches, and folding over the half of each notch. Ornament the lid with leaves and flowers made of paste. Bake it three hours, and see that the oven is not so hot as to scorch it. When done, glaze it all over with white of egg.

This pie will be greatly improved by the addition of some truffles. If you cannot procure truffles, mushrooms cut in pieces may be substituted.

ROASTED PHEASANTS.

Make a stuffing of fresh raw oysters, chopped, and seasoned with pepper, salt, nutmeg, and mace. Mix with it some sweet oil, some yolk of egg, and fill the pheasants with this stuffing. Cover the pheasants with thin slices of bacon or cold ham; wrap them in buttered sheets of white paper, and roast them. Serve them up with oyster sauce.

BROILED QUAILS.

Split the quails down the back, and flatten them. Put them into a stew-pan with sweet-oil, salt, pepper, and a leaf or two of laurel. Cover them with thin slices of bacon or ham, and let them stew slowly on hot coals. When nearly done, take them out, strew over them grated breadcrumbs, and broil them on a gridiron.

Put into the stew-pan a little warm water, and scrape down whatever adheres to the sides; skim it, and let it come to a boil. Pour this gravy into the dish in which you serve up the quails, and lay the bacon round it.

ROASTED PLOVERS.

Scald and pick your plovers, but do not draw them. Lard them, and lay slices of toasted bread in the dripping-pan to receive what falls from the birds while roasting. Serve them up with the toast under them.

Woodcocks and snipes are roasted in the same manner.

PART THE FOURTH

FISH.

STEWED SALMON.

Pour a half-pint of white wine into a stew-pan, with some sliced carrots, onions, and mushrooms; pepper, salt, and mace; and a bunch of chopped sweet-herbs. Lay in your piece of fresh salmon, and pour over it some more wine. Stew it slowly for an hour or more. When done, serve it up with the sauce that is under it, and also with some sauce Mayonnaise in a boat.

The sauce Mayonnaise is made as follows:— Put into a small tureen the yolks of two beaten eggs, a little salt and Cayenne pepper, and a very little vinegar. Stir and mix it well; then add (a drop at a time) two table-spoonfuls of sweet-oil, stirring all the while. When it is well mixed, stir in gradually some more vinegar. To stir and mix it thoroughly will require a quarter of an hour. It will then be very delicate.

You may color it green by adding a little juice of spinach, or some chopped parsley or tarragon at the first, when you put in the eggs.

ROASTED SALMON.

A large piece of fresh salmon is very fine roasted on a spit, first rubbing it with salt, and then basting it all the time with sweet-oil or butter.

For roasted salmon, make a sauce as follows:—Put into a sauce-pan a little parsley, a shalot or small onion, a few mushrooms, and a piece of butter rolled in flour, pepper, salt, and a gill or more of white wine. Let these ingredients boil for half an hour; then strain them through a sieve, and mix with the sauce a table-spoonful of olive-oil.

BROILED SALMON.

Cut several slices of fresh salmon; soak them an hour in a mixture of sweet-oil, chopped parsley, and shalots minced fine, with salt and pepper. Then take each slice with the seasoning on it, and wrap it in buttered paper. Broil the slices on a gridiron. When thoroughly done, take off the paper, and serve up the salmon with melted butter and capers.

Any other large fish may be dressed like salmon.

SALT COD-FISH.

Let it soak twenty-four hours in cold water, which must be changed several times, and every time you change it pour in a wine-glass of vinegar, which will greatly improve the fish. Boil the cod till thoroughly done; then cut the flesh into very small slips; mix it with parsley, butter, vinegar, Cayenne pepper, nutmeg, and mace; add to the mixture some boiled onions, mashed potatoes, and the yolks of two or three beaten eggs. Put the whole mixture into a deep dish, and make it up into the form of a thick round cake. Go all over it with a bunch of feathers, or a small brush, dipped in sweet-oil; and then grate bread crumbs all over it. Set it in the oven till brown. Serve it up, surrounded with triangular or three-cornered slices of toast, dipped in melted butter.

Halibut may be dressed in the same manner, putting salt in the water when you boil it, and also in the seasoning.

Fresh cod may be cooked in the same way.

BROILED FRESH MACKEREL.

Split your mackerel down the back; season it with pepper and salt; cover it all over with oil or butter, and let it lay for half an hour or more; then broil it, pouring on it whatever of the seasoning may be left in the dish.

Serve it up, with sauce in a boat. Let the sauce be of melted butter, with parsley, and a little lemon-juice, or vinegar.

Or you may broil the mackerel whole, having first seasoned it as above, and wrapped it in oiled paper.

BROILED FRESH SHAD.

Having split the shad in half, cover it all over with a seasoning of oil, pepper, salt, chopped onions, parsley, and laurel-leaf. Let it lie an hour or two in the seasoning. Then broil it, covered with the seasoning, and adding a piece of butter.

Or you may cook the shad whole. Make a stuffing of the above ingredients, with the addition of some grated bread; put the stuffing into the shad, and bake it, first pouring over it a glass of white wine.

Any large fresh fish may be baked in the same manner.

HASHED FISH.

Take any sort of cold fish, bone it, and then chop it with the remains of a cold omelet, and some mushrooms if you have them. Mix with it some chopped parsley, a little butter, a slice of bread soaked in milk, and the yolks of two or three hard-boiled eggs chopped fine. Mix all together, and season with pepper and salt. Stew it gently with a little water for half an hour.

LOBSTER PIE.

Having boiled your lobster, take out the meat from the shell, season it with salt, mustard, Cayenne pepper, and vinegar, and beat it well in a mortar. Then stir in a quarter of a pound of butter, the yolks of two beaten eggs, and two ounces or more of grated bread crumbs. Make some puff-paste, put in the mixture, and cover it with a lid of paste ornamented with leaves or flowers of the same. Bake it slowly.

OYSTER LOAVES.

PART THE FIFTH.

VEGETABLES.

STEWED LETTUCE.

Wash a fine lettuce, and tie it up with a string passed several times round it, to keep the leaves together. Put it in boiling water, with a little salt. When the lettuce has boiled, take it out and press it to squeeze out the water, but be careful not to break it.

Having mixed, in a stew-pan, a large spoonful of butter with a spoonful of flour, add half a pint of cream or rich milk; put in the lettuce, with a very little salt, half a nutmeg grated, and two lumps of sugar. Let it boil ten minutes. Take out the lettuce, stir the yolks of two beaten eggs into the sauce, and serve all up together.

STEWED SPINACH.

Take young spinach, and throw it into boiling water with some salt. When it has boiled, take it out, drain it, and lay it in cold water for a quarter of an hour. Then drain it and squeeze it. Cut it small, and put it into a stew-pan, with a large piece of butter. After it has stewed slowly for a quarter of an hour, add a spoonful of flour, with a little salt, sugar, and nutmeg. Moisten it with cream or milk, and let it simmer again over a slow fire for another quarter of an hour. Then serve it up, and lay on it slices of toasted bread dipped in melted butter.

STEWED CUCUMBERS.

Lay your cucumbers in cold water for half an hour; then pare them, and cut them into slips about as long as your little finger; take out the seeds; then boil the cucumbers a few minutes, with a little salt. Take them out, and drain them well.

Put into a stew-pan some butter rolled in flour, and a little cream. Stew your cucumbers in it for ten minutes. When you take them off, stir in the yolks of two beaten eggs; and if you choose, a tea-spoonful of vinegar.

STEWED BEETS.

Boil some beets. Then peel and cut them into slices. Stew them for a quarter of an hour with a piece of butter rolled in flour, some onion and parsley chopped fine, a little vinegar, salt and pepper, and a clove of garlic.

STEWED CARROTS.

Scrape and wash your carrots. Scald them in boiling water; then drain them, and cut them into long slips. Stew them in milk or cream, with a little salt, pepper, and chopped parsley. When done, take them out, stir into the sauce the yolks of one or two eggs, and a lump or two of loaf-sugar, and pour it over the carrots.

STEWED CABBAGE.

Having washed your cabbage, cut it in four, and throw it into boiling water with some salt. When it has boiled till quite tender, take it up, squeeze out the water, and put the cabbage to drain. Then lay it in a stew-pan with butter, salt, pepper, nutmeg, a spoonful of flour, and half a pint of cream. Stew it a quarter of an hour, and pour the sauce over it when you send it to table.

Cauliflowers may be stewed in the same manner.

STEWED PEAS.

Take two quarts of green peas; put them into a stew-pan with a quarter of a pound of butter, a bunch of parsley, and the heart of a fine lettuce cut in pieces, a bunch of mint, three or four lumps of sugar, some salt and pepper, and a very little water. Stir all together, set it on coals and let it stew gently for an hour or an hour and a half. Having taken out the parsley, add a piece of butter rolled in flour; and stir in the yolks of two eggs just before you send it to table.

You may, if you choose, put in the lettuce without cutting it in pieces; tie it up with the bunch of parsley and two onions, and withdraw the whole before you dish the peas. Serve up the lettuce in another dish.

STEWED BEANS.

Put into a stew-pan some parsley and some chives or little onions chopped fine, some mushrooms (if you have them) chopped also, and a large piece of butter rolled in flour. Add a glass of white wine and a little water. Stir all together, and then put in as many beans as will fill a quart measure when strung and cut small; having first soaked them a quarter of an hour in cold water. Let them stew gently on hot coals till quite tender. Just before you serve them up, stir in the yolks of two eggs. You may substitute for the wine a tumbler of cream, but it must be stirred in at the last.

STEWED ONIONS.

Boil some small onions with salt, and then drain them. Lay them in a stew-pan with a piece of butter, and sprinkle them with flour, pepper and salt. Pour on them some cream, and then turn every onion with a spoon. Stew them ten minutes, and serve them up.

ONIONS STEWED IN WINE.

Boil twenty or thirty onions a quarter of an hour with a bunch of sweet herbs, some salt, a few cloves, and a laurel leaf. Then take out the onions, and put them into a stew-pan with some salt, a piece of butter rolled in flour, and a pint of red wine. Stew them another quarter of an hour, and serve them up garnished with pieces of toast dipped in the sauce.

STEWED MUSHROOMS.

Having peeled and washed your mushrooms, drain them, and stew them with butter, pepper, salt, and a little chopped parsley, adding a little flour and warm water. When they are done, stir into the sauce the yolks of two or three eggs, and some cream. Toast and butter a slice of bread. Lay it on the dish under the mushrooms, and pour the sauce over them.

Put in a small onion with the mushrooms, that you may know by its turning almost black, whether there is a poisonous one among them. If the onion turns black, throw away all the mushrooms.

STEWED POTATOES.

Boil eight or nine large potatoes with a little salt, and then peel and cut them in slices. Put into a stew-pan a large piece of butter, a spoonful of flour, some salt, and half a grated nutmeg. Add a half-pint of cream, and mix all together. When this sauce boils, put in your sliced potatoes, and let them stew a quarter of an hour.

STEWED POTATOES WITH TURNIPS.

Pare and boil an equal quantity of turnips and potatoes. When done, drain and mash them. Melt some butter in a stew-pan, and add to it a little mustard. Stew the mixed potatoes and turnips in it, with a small quantity of hot milk, for about ten minutes.

ASPARAGUS WITH CREAM.

Wash and boil four or five bundles of asparagus. Have ready a pint of cream, or a pint of milk, with the yolks of six eggs stirred into it. Take four large rolls of bread, and cut a round piece out of the top of each. Scoop out the crumb from the inside of the rolls, and put it into the cream with the heads of the asparagus, of which you must save out a sufficient number (with a small piece of the stalk left on each) to stick the rolls with. Make holes in the top-pieces of the rolls.

Fry the rolls in butter. Put the most of the asparagus heads into the cream mixed with the crumb of the rolls, and simmer it awhile over a slow fire. When the rolls are fried, fill their cavities with the mixture. Stick the tops with the remainder of the asparagus, and lay them on the rolls.

Asparagus may be simply boiled with salt, and served up on toasted bread dipped in oil, and eaten with oil sauce.

POTATOES STEWED WHOLE.

Boil two dozen small new potatoes, with some salt. Put into a stew-pan a piece of butter rolled in flour, half the peel of a lemon grated, half a nutmeg grated, some salt, two or three lumps of sugar, and three tea-spoonfuls of sweet oil. Lay the potatoes in this mixture, squeeze over them the juice of a lemon, and let them stew gently about ten minutes.

FRIED POTATOES.

Make a batter with the yolks of three eggs, a little salt, a table-spoonful of oil, a table-spoonful of brandy, and sufficient flour or grated bread to thicken it. Have ready some large cold potatoes cut in slices. Dip each slice in the batter, and fry them in butter.

FRIED CAULIFLOWER.

Wash a fine large cauliflower, and cut it into quarters. Having boiled some water with salt, throw the cauliflower into it, and boil it till you can nip it easily with your fingers. Take it out and drain it. Then put it into a pan with salt, pepper and vinegar, and let it lie half an hour, turning it frequently.

Make the following batter, which must be prepared half an hour or more before it is wanted, that it may have time to rise. Take three table-spoonfuls of flour, three beaten eggs, a table-spoonful of butter melted in a little warm water, a spoonful of sweet oil, and a spoonful of brandy. Stir all together; and if you find it too thin, add a little more flour; cover it, and let it set half an hour. Then beat to a stiff froth the whites of the eggs, and stir them hard into the batter. Dip your quarters of cauliflower into this mixture, and fry them of a fine light brown.

When the cauliflower is done, let it remain in the pan a quarter of an hour before you send it to table. Lay fried parsley round it.

Broccoli may be fried in the same manner.

FRIED CELERY.

Take ten or twelve fine stalks of celery. Cut them into pieces about six inches long, and lay them an hour in salt and water. Drain them, spread them on a dish, and sprinkle them with powdered sugar. Make a batter of eggs, milk, and grated bread; allowing four eggs to a pint of milk. Dip each piece of celery into the batter, and fry them in butter.

BROILED MUSHROOMS. [71-*]

Peel, wash, and drain your mushrooms, and then cut them in pieces. Make a square case of white paper, and butter it well. Fill it with the mushrooms mixed with butter, salt, and pepper. Broil them on the gridiron over a clear fire, and serve them up in the paper.

If you choose, you may mix with the mushrooms some chopped onion and sweet-herbs.

STUFFED CABBAGE. (CHOUX FARCIS.)

Take a large cabbage, with a hard full head; put it into boiling water with some salt, and let it boil from five to ten minutes. Then take it out and drain it. Cut off the stalk close to the bottom, so that the cabbage may stand upright on the dish, and then carefully take out the inside leaves or heart; leaving the outside leaves whole.

Chop fine what you have taken out of the inside, and chop also some cold ham and veal, or cold chicken. Likewise four eggs boiled hard. Mix together the chopped eggs, the ham and veal, the cabbage heart, and some grated bread, adding salt and pepper. Fill the cabbage with this stuffing, and tie tape round it to keep the outside leaves together. Then put it into a deep stew-pan, with a quarter of a pound of butter rolled in flour, and an onion stuck full of cloves. Let it simmer over a slow fire for two hours or more.

When it is done, take off the tape, set the cabbage upright in a dish, and pour melted butter over it.

Lettuce may be done in the same manner.

STUFFED POTATOES.

Take eight very large potatoes, wash and pare them. Make a small slit or incision in each of them, and scoop out carefully with a knife as much of the inside as will leave all round a shell about the thickness of two cents. Then make a force-meat of the substance you have taken out of the inside, mixing it with two minced onions, a small piece of minced cold ham or pork, about two ounces of butter, and a little parsley; adding the yolks of two or three beaten eggs. Mix the stuffing thoroughly, by pounding it in a mortar.

Butter the inside of the potatoes, and fill them with this mixture. Then having buttered a large dish, lay your potatoes in it separately. Bake them half an hour, or till they are of a fine brown.

When you mash potatoes, moisten them with milk or cream, adding a little salt. Heap them up on the dish in the form of a pyramid. Smooth the sides of the pyramid with the back of a spoon, and brown it by holding over it a red-hot shovel.

STUFFED CUCUMBERS.

Cut off one end of each of the cucumbers, and scoop out all the seeds with a fork. Then pare them. Prepare a stuffing made of bread crumbs, cold meat minced, salt, pepper, and sweet-herbs. Fill your cucumbers with it, and fasten on with a skewer the pieces you have cut off from their ends. Sow up every one separately in a thin cloth. Put them into a pan with butter, flour, a bunch of sweet-herbs, and a little warm water. Let them stew very slowly for about two hours, and then take them out. Remove the cloths, and serve up the cucumbers with the sauce under them.

STUFFED TOMATAS.

Scoop out the inside of a dozen large tomatas, without spoiling their shape. Pass the inside through a sieve, and then mix it with grated bread, chopped sweet-herbs, nutmeg, salt, and pepper. Stew it ten minutes, with a laurel leaf, or two peach leaves. Remove the leaves, and stuff the tomatas with the mixture, tying a string round each to keep them in shape. Sprinkle them all over with rasped bread-crust. Set them in a buttered dish, and bake them in an oven. Take off the strings, and serve up the tomatas.

Egg-plants may be cooked in the same manner.

CAULIFLOWERS WITH CHEESE.

Having washed and boiled your cauliflowers in salt and water, drain them well. Make a white sauce in a small pan, with butter rolled in flour, and a little milk. Pour some of this sauce into the bottom of a dish that will bear the fire. Chop your cauliflower, and spread a layer of it on the sauce. Then cover it with a layer of rich cheese, grated and slightly sprinkled with pepper. Then spread on the remainder of the cauliflower, and then another layer of peppered cheese, and so on till your dish is nearly full. Pour over it the rest of the sauce. Prepare two or three handfuls of grated bread, mixed with a little of the grated cheese. Spread it all over the surface of the last layer of cauliflower, and smooth it with the back of a spoon. Allow a quarter of a pound of cheese to each cauliflower.

Put the dish in a slow oven about a quarter of an hour before you serve it up, and bake it till a brown crust forms on the outside. Clear off the butter from the edges of the dish, and send it to table hot.

Broccoli may be done in the same manner.

RAGOOED CABBAGE.

Wash a fine savoy cabbage, and boil it for half an hour in salt and water. Then take it out, drain it, and lay it for ten minutes in cold water. Afterwards squeeze and drain it well, and take out the stalk. Chop the cabbage slightly, and put it into a stew-pan with a quarter of a pound of butter, and add two table-spoonfuls of flour. Season it with salt and pepper, and moisten it with a little water. Let it stew slowly for an hour, and then serve it up.

Cauliflowers or broccoli may be done in the same manner.

RAGOOED MUSHROOMS.

Take a pint of fresh mushrooms. When they are peeled and the stalks cut off, put the mushrooms into a stew-pan with two table-spoonfuls of vinegar, a sprig or two of parsley, a small onion, a few chives chopped fine, some salt, pepper, and grated nutmeg. Let it boil gently for a quarter of an hour. Before it goes to table, stir in the yolks of two eggs.

If the onion has turned blue or black, throw the whole away, as it is evident that some poisonous ones are among the mushrooms.

PURÉES.

The word Purée cannot be exactly translated, as there is nothing in the English language that gives precisely the same idea. In French it is generally applied to a certain manner of cooking vegetables that converts them into a substance resembling marmalade, which, when the coarser parts are strained out, leaves a fine smooth jelly.

It is served up with meat.

PURÉE OF TURNIPS.

Wash and pare some of the finest turnips. Cut them into small pieces, and let them lie for half an hour in cold water. Then take them out and drain them. Put them into a stew-pan, with a large piece of butter and some salt and pepper. Moisten them with a little broth or boiling water. Let them stew over a very slow fire, for five or six hours, stirring them frequently. Then rub them through a sieve, and serve up the jelly with roast meat.

PURÉE OF CELERY.

Wash your celery, peel it, and stew it slowly for three or four hours, with salt, and a very little water. Then pass it through a sieve, and season it with pepper, salt, and nutmeg to your taste.

PURÉE OF ONIONS.

Take thirty onions; cut them in slices and put them into a stew-pan, with a little salt, pepper, and a grated nutmeg. Let them stew slowly till they are of a fine brown color, and then add a table-spoonful of broth or warm water.

When it has attained the proper consistence, strain it and serve it up.

PURÉE OF MUSHROOMS.

Peel a pint of mushrooms, cut them in pieces, and put them in a pan with as much cold water as will keep them from burning. Throw in with them a small onion to test their goodness; as, if there is a bad or poisonous one among them, the onion will turn of a bluish black while cooking. In that case, throw them all away.

Stew them slowly till they have lost all shape and have become an undistinguishable mass. Then strain them.

Put into a stew-pan a large piece of butter, or a spoonful of flour, and two lumps of sugar. Add your purée, and let it stew again for about five minutes. When you take it off the fire, stir in the yolks of two eggs slightly beaten, and a spoonful of cream or rich milk. Put it in the middle of a dish, and lay round it thin slices of fried bread or toast.

PURÉE OF BEANS.

Having strung and cut your beans till you have a quart, throw them into boiling water, with a little salt. Let them remain a quarter of an hour. Then drain them, and throw into cold water to green them. After they have lain half an hour in the cold water, take them out and drain them again.

Put a large piece of butter into a stew-pan with some pepper, a little salt, and a spoonful of flour. Add your beans, and cover them with broth or warm water. Put in a bunch of sweet-herbs cut small, and stew the whole very slowly till it has dissolved into a mass. Then strain it. Put a piece of butter into the purée, and serve it up.

PURÉE OF GREEN PEAS.

Take a quart of shelled green peas. Wash them, and put them into a stew-pan with water enough to cover them, a little salt and pepper, a piece of butter the size of a walnut, a laurel leaf or a couple of peach-leaves, and a bunch of mint.

Let them stew very slowly; and if necessary moisten them occasionally with a little warm water or broth. Stir them frequently, that they may not stick to the pan. When they become of the consistence of marmalade, strain it. Chop an onion fine, fry it in butter, and have it ready to mix with the purée.

Dried split peas may be made into a purée in the same manner.

Purées may be made in a similar manner of different sorts of meat, poultry &c. seasoned, stewed slowly to a jelly, then strained through a cullender or sieve, and taken as soups.

71-* In gathering mushrooms, take only those that are of a pale pink color underneath, and a dull white or pearl color on the top. Those that are perfectly white above, or whose under side is white, yellow, or any color but pale pink, are unfit to eat, and poisonous.

After being gathered awhile, the pink tinge changes to brown, but it always appears on the good ones while in the ground.

EGGS, &c.

In choosing eggs, hold them up against the light, and if you see that the yolk is round, and the white thin and clear, you may suppose them to be good. But if the yolk appears to be broken and mixed with the white, giving it a thick cloudy look, you may be sure that the egg is bad. Eggs may be preserved by keeping them in a keg of lime-water, or by greasing each egg all over with dripping, and putting them into a tight vessel filled with wood-ashes, placing them all with their small ends downwards. You may also keep them by burying them in salt. Still they are never so good as when quite fresh.

When you break eggs for use, do every one separately, in a saucer. If you find the egg good, throw it into the pan in which they are to be beaten. If you meet with a bad one, throw it away and wash the saucer or get a clean one. A single bad egg will make the whole mixture heavy, spungy, and of an unpleasant taste.

BOILED EGGS.

When the water boils hard, put in the eggs, and let them boil exactly three minutes. Then take them out, and cover them up for about a minute, which will greatly improve them. Send them to table wrapped in a napkin, and laid in a deep dish.

FRIED EGGS.

Melt a piece of butter in a frying-pan. When it ceases to hiss, put in the yolks only of your eggs. Season them with pepper and salt. When fried, color them by holding over them a red-hot shovel.

STEWED EGGS.

Melt some butter in a dish that will bear the fire. Add to it salt, and nutmeg, and a little milk in the proportion of a table-spoonful to each egg. Mix them well together. Then lay over it the yolks of your eggs, first ascertaining that they are all good. Let it stew over a slow fire for a few minutes; and color it by holding over it a red-hot shovel. The eggs must not be allowed to get hard, but the surface should be soft and perfectly smooth and even.

Before you put in the eggs, you may stir into the mixture some heads of boiled asparagus.

STUFFED EGGS.

Boil twelve eggs hard. Take off the shell, and cut each egg in half. Take out the yolks, and pound them in a mortar with a quarter of a pound of butter; a nutmeg; some grated bread that has been soaked in milk; a little salt; and if you choose, some minced sweet-herbs. Fill the whites of the eggs with this stuffing, heaping it up, and smoothing it into a round even shape. Butter a dish, and spread over the inside a thin layer of the stuffing. Arrange in it all your halves of eggs, the bottoms downwards. Put them into an oven, the lid of which must be hot. Let them set about five minutes, and then send them to table.

EGG SNOW.

Take a quart of milk, and stir into it two spoonfuls of rose-water, and a quarter of a pound of white sugar, with a powdered nutmeg. Add by degrees the yolks of twelve eggs well beaten. Boil the whole together, stirring it all the time, so as to make a thick smooth custard. If you keep it too long on the fire, it will be lumpy. Set it away to get cold in a deep dish. Beat the whites of the eggs to a stiff froth that will stand alone, adding to it twelve drops of essence of lemon. Heap it on the dish of custard so as to look like a pile of snow; or you may drop it with a large spoon, so as to form separate balls. On the top of each ball you may lay a tea-spoonful of stiff currant-jelly.

PANCAKES.

Beat together a quart of sifted flour, six eggs, a table-spoonful of brandy, a grated nutmeg, a little salt, and sufficient water to make a thin batter. Melt a piece of butter in a frying-pan, or substitute a little sweet-oil. Pour in a ladleful of the batter, and let it spread into a circular form. When it is slightly brown on one side, turn it carefully on the other. Serve them up with white sugar grated over each.

You may color them pink, by stirring into the mixture some of the juice of a beet-root, which has been boiled and then beaten in a mortar.

OMELETS.

Cheese Omelet.—Grate some rich cheese, and mix it gradually with your eggs while beating them. Season with salt and pepper. Melt some butter in a frying-pan. Put in your omelet, and fry it first on one side, and then on the other. When you dish it up, fold it over in half.

Bread Omelet.—Put two handfuls or more of bread crumbs into half a pint of cream, with a grated nutmeg and a little salt. When the bread has absorbed all the cream, stir it into the eggs as you beat them for the omelet. Fry it in butter, and when dished, fold one half over the other.

Lobster Omelet.—Beat in a mortar the flesh of a boiled lobster, adding, at times, a little butter; and season it with pepper and salt. Stir it gradually into the eggs while beating them. Fry it in butter.

Onion Omelet.—Boil some onions; mince them fine, and moisten them with milk. Stir them into the eggs as you beat them.

Ham Omelet.—Is made with grated cold ham, stirred into the eggs while beating.

Omelets may be seasoned in the same manner with parsley, chopped sweet-herbs, or mushrooms. Also with minced oysters.

MACCARONI.

Boil half a pound of maccaroni with two ounces of butter, some whole pepper, and a little salt. Do not let it boil long enough for the maccaroni to lose its shape. When done, mix with it a quarter of a pound of rich cheese, scraped or grated. Butter a deep dish, and put the mixture into it. Then set it for a quarter of an hour in the oven. Brown the top with a red-hot shovel.

MACCARONI PIE.

Take half a pound of maccaroni, and put it into a stew-pan with an ounce of butter, a little salt and pepper, and water enough to cover it. Stew it till dry. Then grate a quarter of a pound of fine cheese, and mix it with the maccaroni, adding another ounce of butter. Set it away to get cold.

Take another pan, which must be very deep, with a flat bottom, and nearly the shape of a drum. Butter the inside. Make a good paste, and cover with it the whole interior of the pan, sides and bottom. Put in the maccaroni. Cover the pie with a lid of paste. Bake it at least half an hour. When done, loosen it from the pan and turn it out on a dish. It will be in the form of a drum, if the pan was of that shape.

BLANCMANGE IN EGGS.

Take two ounces of shelled sweet almonds, and one ounce of shelled bitter almonds. Blanch them by throwing them into scalding water to make the skins peel off easily; then put them in cold water; wipe them dry afterwards, and pound them in a mortar, adding at times a little rose-water.

Dissolve an ounce of isinglass in warm water, and then stir it into a quart of cream. Add a quarter of a pound of broken loaf-sugar, and a wine-glass of rose-water. Boil it hard for a quarter of an hour, and stir it all the time. Then strain it through a linen bag, and put it into egg-cups, or into the halves of egg-shells nicely and evenly trimmed, and set it away in a cold place to congeal.

PART THE SIXTH.

PASTRY, CAKES, &c.

FRENCH PASTE.

Sift a quart of flour, and lay it in a pan. Make a hole in the middle, and put into it the white of an egg slightly beaten, a piece of butter the size of an egg, and a very little salt. Pour in gradually as much cold water as will moisten it. Mix it well with your hands, as rapidly as possible, and see that no lumps are left in it. Set it away to cool, and in a quarter of an hour roll it out, and spread over it half a pound of butter which has been kept in ice. Then fold up the paste with the four sides laid one over another, so as entirely to inclose the butter, and set it for half an hour in a cool place. Then roll it again; fold it, and give it another roll. Set it away again; and in half an hour roll it out twice more, and it will be fit for use.

PUFF PASTE.

May be made with a pound of butter, and a pound and a quarter of sifted flour. The butter must be washed in cold water, and then squeezed very hard, and made up into a lump. Divide it into eight parts. Mix one part of the butter with the flour, adding just enough of water to moisten it. Roll it out; spread over it a second portion of the butter; flour it; fold it up, and roll it out again, adding another division of the butter. Repeat this till you get in all the butter, a piece at a time, folding and rolling the paste with each separate portion of the butter. Then set it away to cool. If it sets several hours, it will be the better for it; and better still if the paste is made the night before it is wanted; always keeping it in a cold place.

While buttering and rolling, do every thing as quickly as possible.

Before you put it into the dishes, roll it out once more. It is difficult in warm weather to make good puff paste without a marble table, or slab, to roll it on.

CREAM TARTS.

Mix together a quart of flour, half a pound of butter, a little salt, and two beaten eggs. Add a little cold water; make it into a paste, and set it away to cool. Then roll it out again. Cut it into round shapes with the edge of a tumbler. Lay round each a rim made of an even strip of the paste, and notch it handsomely. Bake them for a quarter of an hour, and then take them from the oven. Beat together a pint of cream, four eggs, and four table-spoonfuls of powdered sugar. Fill the tarts with this mixture, grate nutmeg over each, and bake them again for a quarter of an hour.

ALMOND TARTS.

Blanch half a pound of shelled sweet almonds and three ounces of shelled bitter almonds. Beat them, a few at a time, in a mortar, mixing them well, and adding at times a little rose-water. When done, mix with them a quarter of a pound of loaf-sugar powdered, and the juice and grated peel of half a lemon.

Have ready some fine paste. Cut it into circular pieces about the size and thickness of a dollar. Put into each piece of paste some of the almond mixture, heaping it up in the centre. Cover them with lids of the same, and crimp the edges very neatly. Bake them about half an hour, and grate sugar over them when done.

RISSOLES.

Make some fine paste, and cut it out with the edge of a tumbler. Have ready some minced veal, seasoned in the best manner, or some chopped oysters, or any sort of force-meat, and lay some of it on one half of each piece of paste. Then turn over it the other half, so as to inclose the meat. Crimp the edges. Put some butter into a frying-pan. Lay the rissoles into it, and fry them of a light brown.

They should be in the shape of a half-moon.

ALMOND CUSTARDS.

Blanch and pound in a mortar half a pound of shelled sweet almonds, and three ounces of peach-kernels, or shelled bitter almonds, adding sufficient rose-water to moisten them. When they are all pounded to a paste, mix with them a quarter of a pound of powdered loaf-sugar, and boil them in a quart of milk or cream. Then set it away to cool. When cold, stir eight beaten eggs into it. Put the mixture into cups. Set them in an iron oven half filled with water, and bake them.

VANILLA CUSTARDS.

Cut a vanilla bean into slips, and boil them in a quart of milk, with a quarter of a pound of white sugar. Let it boil slowly for a quarter of an hour, and then set it away to cool. When cold, stir into it eight beaten eggs, having left out the whites of four. Put the mixture into cups, set them in water and bake them. Color them when done, by holding over them a red-hot shovel. When cold, grate on sugar.

Lemon Custards are made in the same manner; substituting for the vanilla bean the grated rind of a large fresh lemon.

CHOCOLATE CUSTARDS.

Cut into pieces half a pound of the best chocolate. Pour on it sufficient milk to prevent its burning, and let it boil ten minutes. After you remove it from the fire, have ready a pint of boiling milk or cream, and pour it on the chocolate. Beat together the yolks of eight eggs and the whites of two only, and stir them into the chocolate with two ounces, or more, of loaf-sugar. Put the mixture into cups, set them in an oven with water in it, and bake them.

Beat the six remaining whites of eggs to a froth, adding a very little sugar, and heap some of the froth on each custard. You may lay on the top of each heap of froth one of the bonbons or confections called chocolate-nuts.

COFFEE CUSTARDS.

Take two ounces of roasted coffee and two ounces of raw coffee. Pound them together in a mortar, but do not grind them. Boil this coffee in a quart of rich milk. Let it get cold, and then strain it. Stir into it two ounces of powdered loaf-sugar, and two large spoonfuls of cream. Beat eight eggs, omitting the whites of four. Stir them gradually into the coffee. Put it into cups, and bake the custards in an oven with water. Grate white sugar over the tops when cold.

TEA CUSTARDS.

Boil a quart of cream or rich milk, and pour it (while boiling) on three ounces of the best green tea. Add two ounces of loaf sugar. Cover it and set it away. Take eight eggs, and beat them well, leaving out the whites of four; and when the tea is cold, stir in the eggs. Then strain the whole mixture; put it into cups, and bake them in an oven with water. Grate sugar over the top of each.

RICE POTTAGE.

Put six table-spoonfuls of rice into a pint of water, and boil it till quite soft. Drain it through a sieve, and put the rice into a quart of milk with a quarter of a pound of sugar, and three or four peach-leaves, or a few peach-kernels. Boil it, and before you serve it up, take out the peach-leaves or kernels, and stir in the yolks of two eggs.

APPLE FRITTERS.

Pare and core some fine large pippins, and cut them into round slices. Soak them in brandy for two or three hours. Make a batter, in the proportion of four eggs to a table-spoonful of olive-oil, a table spoonful of rose-water, the same quantity of brandy, the same quantity of cold water. Thicken the batter with a sufficient quantity of flour stirred in by degrees, and mix it two or three hours before it is wanted, that it may be light by fermentation.

Put some butter into a frying-pan. Dip each slice of apple into the batter, and fry them brown. Then drain them, grate white sugar over them, and send them to table.

Peach Fritters may be made in the same way, but the peaches must be cut into quarters.

BREAD FRITTERS.

Boil a quart of milk with cinnamon and sugar to your taste. When done, stir in a table-spoonful of rose-water. Cut some slices of bread into a circular shape. Soak them in the milk till they have absorbed it. Then drain them. Have ready some yolks of eggs well beaten. Dip the slices of bread into it, and fry them in butter. Serve them up strewed with powdered sugar.

RICE CAKE.

Take half a pound of rice and wash it well. Put it into a pint of cream or milk, and boil it soft. Let it get cold. Then stir into it alternately a quarter of a pound of sugar, two ounces of butter, eight eggs well beaten (having left out the whites of four), and a wine-glass of rose-water, or else the grated peel of a lemon. Mix all well. Butter a mould or a deep pan with straight sides, and spread grated bread crumbs all over its inside. Put in the mixture, and bake it three quarters of an hour.

Ground rice is best for this cake.

If any of the cake is left, you may next day cut it in slices and fry them in butter.

Or, instead of baking the mixture in a large cake, you may put flour on your hands, and roll it into round balls. Make a batter of beaten eggs, sugar, and grated bread; dip the balls into it, and fry them in butter.

POTATO CAKE.

Roast in the ashes a dozen small or six large potatoes. When done, peel them, and put them into a pan with a little salt, and the rind of a lemon grated. Add a quarter of a pound of butter, or half a pint of cream, and a quarter of a pound of sugar. Having mashed the potatoes with this mixture, rub it through a cullender, and stir it very hard. Then set it away to cool.

Beat eight eggs, and stir them gradually into the mixture. Season it with a tea-spoonful of mixed spice, and half a glass of rose-water.

Butter a mould or a deep dish, and spread the inside all over with grated bread. Put in the mixture, and bake it for three quarters of an hour.

SPONGE CAKE—CALLED IN FRANCE BISCUIT.

Take ten eggs, and beat them till very thick and smooth. Add gradually a pound of powdered loaf-sugar. Rub a lump of loaf-sugar all over the rind of a large lemon, to draw the juice to the surface; then grate the peel of the lemon, and stir it into the mixture, together with the lump of sugar. Squeeze in the juice of the lemon, and add two table-spoonfuls of rose-water. Beat the mixture very hard; then take half a pound of potato flour (which is best), or else of fine wheat flour, and stir it in very lightly and slowly. It must be baked immediately.

Have ready some small square or oblong cases of thick white paper, with an edge turned up all round, and sewed at the corners. They should be about a finger in length, half a finger in breadth, and an inch and a half in depth. Either butter these paper-cases, or sift white sugar all over the inside. Put some of the mixture into each case, but do not fill them to the top. Grate loaf-sugar over the top of each, and bake them quickly.

These cakes are much better when baked in paper cases; tins being generally too thick for them. No cake requires greater care in baking. If the oven is not hot enough, both at top and bottom, they will fall and be heavy, and lose their shape.

CROQUETTES.

Take a pound of powdered sugar, a pound of butter, half a pound of wheat-flour, and half a pound of Indian meal; mix all together, and add the juice and grated peel of a large lemon, with spice to your taste. Make it into a lump of paste. Then put it into a mortar, and beat it hard on all sides.

Roll it out thin, and cut it into cakes with the edge of a tumbler, or with a tin cutter.

Flour a shallow tin pan. Lay the cakes into it, but not close together. Bake them about ten minutes. Grate sugar over them when done.

MARGUERITES.

Beat together till very light, a pound of butter and a pound of powdered sugar. Sift a pound of flour into a pan. Take the yolks only, of twelve eggs, and beat them till very thick and smooth. Pour them into the flour, and add the beaten butter and sugar. Stir in a grated nutmeg, and a wine-glass of rose-water. Mix the whole together, till it becomes a lump of dough.

Flour your paste-board, and lay the dough upon it; sprinkle it with flour. Roll it out about half an inch thick, and cut it into round cakes with the edge of a cup. Flour a shallow pan, put in the cakes (so as not to touch), and bake them about five minutes in a quick oven. If the oven is too cool, they will run.

When the cakes are cool, lay on each a large lump of currant jelly. Take the whites of the eggs, and beat them till they stand alone. Then add to them, by degrees, sufficient powdered sugar to make the consistence of icing, and ten drops of strong essence of lemon. Heap on each cake, with a spoon, a pile of the icing over the currant-jelly. Set them in a cool oven till the icing becomes firm and of a pale brownish tint.

These cakes are very fine.

WAFERS.

Sift half a pound of flour into a pan. Make a hole in the middle, and put in three beaten eggs, a table-spoonful of brandy, a table-spoonful of powdered sugar, a table-spoonful of sweet-oil, and a very little salt, not more than will lie on a sixpence. Mix all together, adding gradually a little milk, till you have a batter about the thickness of good cream. Then stir in a table-spoonful of rose-water. Let there be no lumps in the batter. Heat your wafer-iron on both sides, in a clear fire, but do not allow it to get red-hot. Then grease the inside with a brush dipped in sweet-oil, or a clean rag with some butter tied up in it. Then put in the batter, allowing about two table-spoonfuls to each wafer. Close the iron, and in baking turn it first on one side and then on the other. When done, sprinkle the wafers with powdered sugar, and roll each one up, pressing the edges together while warm, so as to make them unite.

A little practice will soon show you the proper degree of heat, and the time necessary for baking the wafers. They should be but slightly colored, and of an even tint all over.

GINGERBREAD.

Mix together two pounds of flour, one pound of sugar, five beaten eggs, three quarters of a pound of butter, and a tea-cupful of ginger. Put the flour to the other ingredients, a little at a time, and stir the whole very hard. Melt a tea-spoonful of sal aratus or fine pearl-ash in a little sour milk, and stir it in at the last. Roll the dough into sheets, and cut it out with square tins. If not stiff enough for rolling, add a little more flour. Lay it in buttered pans, and bake it in a moderate oven.

PART THE SEVENTH.

PREPARATIONS OF FRUIT, SUGAR, &c.

AN APPLE CHARLOTTE.

Pare and core some fine pippins, and cut them into small pieces. Melt some butter in the bottom of a pan. Then lay your apples in it with a sufficient proportion of sugar, beaten cinnamon or nutmeg, and some rose-water or grated lemon-peel. Set the pan in an oven, and let the apples bake till they are quite soft. Then take them out of the pan, and mash them to a marmalade with the back of a spoon.

Cut some thin slices of bread into a triangular or three-cornered shape, and dip them in melted butter. Then butter a broad deep dish, and lay the pieces of bread in the bottom of it, making the points meet in the centre. Spread a thick layer of apple all over the bread; then more bread, covered with another layer of apple, and so on till the dish is full; having a cover of bread on the top. Set it in the oven, and bake it slowly about a quarter of an hour.

A very fine Charlotte may be made by substituting slices of spunge-cake for the bread, or having square spunge-cakes laid round, leaving a hole in the centre to be filled up with gooseberry jelly. If you use spunge-cake, you need not put it in the oven.

APPLE COMPOTE.

Pare and core some large pippins, but leave them whole. Make a syrup by boiling and skimming a pound of loaf-sugar melted in a gill of water, into which the half of the white of an egg has been beaten. When the syrup is quite clear, boil the apples in it till soft and tender. Then take them out, lay them in a deep dish, and fill up with small sweet-meats or marmalade the holes from whence you took the cores.

Boil the syrup again till it becomes a jelly. Pour it hot over your apples, and set it in a cool place to congeal.

The syrup will be much improved by adding to it the juice of one or two lemons, or a dozen drops of essence of lemon.

COMPOTE OF PEARS.

Pare them, but leave on the stems. Lay them in a preserving-pan; and to a dozen moderate-sized pears, put half a pound of white sugar, a gill of water, and a few sticks of cinnamon, with some slips of lemon-peel. Simmer them till tender; and when half done, pour in a glass of port-wine. When quite done, take out the pears and lay them in a deep dish. Strain the syrup; give it another boil, and pour it over them.

COMPOTE OF CHESTNUTS.

Take some of the largest and finest chestnuts. Cut a slit in the shell of each, and roast them in a charcoal furnace, taking care not to burn them. When done, peel them and put them into a pan with some powdered sugar, and a very little water. Let them simmer over a slow fire for about a quarter of an hour. When done, take them out, put them into a dish, squeeze over them some lemon-juice, and sprinkle them with powdered sugar.

FRIED APPLES.

Pare and core some of the largest and finest pippins, and cut them into thin round slices. Mix together in a deep dish some brandy, lemon-juice, and powdered sugar. Lay the slices of apple in it, and let them soak for several hours. Then drain them, and dip each slice in flour. Put some butter into a pan, and fry the apples of a fine brown. Dish them, and grate loaf-sugar over them.

Quinces may be done in the same manner. So also may peaches, but they must be cut in half.

PEACH MARMALADE.

Take ripe peaches; pare them and cut them in half, taking out the stones. Weigh them, and to each pound of fruit allow half a pound of loaf-sugar. Mash them with the sugar, and put them in a preserving-kettle. Boil them slowly till they become a shapeless mass, which will generally be in about three quarters of an hour. Stir the marmalade frequently, to prevent its sticking to the kettle. Blanch half the kernels, and cut them in two; and when the marmalade is about half done, put them into it to give it a fine flavor. Take out the kernels when the marmalade is cold, and then tie it up in pots or glasses, laying over it paper dipped in brandy.

Marmalade of plums or green-gages may be made in the same manner.

BRANDY PEACHES.

Take large yellow free-stone peaches; they must not be too ripe. Wipe off the down with a flannel, and then prick each peach to the stone with a large pin. Put them into a pan, and scald them with boiling water. Cover them, and let them rest for a few minutes. This is to make them white. You may repeat the scalding two or three times. Then take them out to drain and dry.

Allow a pound of the best loaf-sugar to a dozen large peaches. Put the sugar into a preserving-kettle (lined with enamel or porcelain), and melt it, allowing to each pound a gill of water, and half the white of an egg. Boil the sugar, and skim it till perfectly clear. Then put in the peaches, and give them a boil. Take them off the fire, and let them set in the syrup till next day.

The following morning take out the peaches, set the syrup over the fire, and when it has boiled a few minutes put in the peaches, and give them a short boil. Then take them out, and let them get cold. Boil down the syrup to half its original quantity, but take care that it does not boil long enough to congeal or become thick. Put the peaches into a glass jar, and pour the syrup over them. Fill up the jar with brandy, and cover it closely.

Apricots may be done in the same manner. Also pears. The stems must be left on the pears.

GOOSEBERRY POTTAGE.

Stew two quarts of fine large gooseberries in just sufficient water to cover them. When quite soft and broken, mash them with the back of a spoon, make them very sweet with sugar, and set them away to get cold. Take three pints of rich milk; stir into it a pounded nutmeg and the yolks of four eggs. Then set it over a bed of hot coals, and let it simmer, stirring it gently all the time. Before it comes to a boil, take it off the fire and gradually stir in the gooseberries. It must be quite cold before you serve it up. Send it to table in a bowl, and eat spunge-cake with it.

It will be still nicer, if you use the pulp only of the gooseberries, pressed through a sieve or cullender.

FRUIT JELLIES.

Previous to making your jelly, clarify the sugar, which must be the best loaf. Break it up, and to each pound allow a gill of water and an ounce of isinglass. Mix the water with the sugar. Dissolve the isinglass in as much hot water as will cover it. Set the sugar over the fire in a preserving-kettle; and when it is beginning to boil, throw in the melted isinglass. Skim the syrup well, and when it is quite clear and no more scum rises, take it from the fire, cover it, and leave it to settle.

Prepare the fruit of which you intend to make the jelly. If small fruit, such as gooseberries, currants, grapes, raspberries, or strawberries; pick them from the stems, and put them into a jar; set the jar in a vessel of warm water, and let them come to a boil. Then take them out, put them into a fine sieve, set a pan under it, and with the back of a large spoon press out all the juice from the fruit. Mix the juice, while warm, with the clarified sugar, and boil them together for about a quarter of an hour. Then put it into your jars or glasses, and tie it up with brandy-paper.

If you want the jelly for immediate use, put it into a mould; set the mould in ice for two or three hours; and when the jelly is congealed, loosen it by setting the mould in warm water, and then turn it out.

PRESERVED PUMPKIN.

Take a fine ripe pumpkin of a deep rich color. Cut from it as many slices as you want; they should be very thin. Have ready some lime-water. Put into it the slices of pumpkin, and let them soak for twenty-four hours. Then take them out, wash them well in cold water, and wipe them dry. Having prepared a nicely clarified syrup of sugar, put the slices of pumpkin into it, and let them simmer over a slow fire without stirring, for a day and a night; but first flavor them to your taste with lemon-juice mixed into the syrup. When done, they will be crisp and transparent. Put them into broad stone or queensware pots, and tie them up with brandy-paper.

PRESERVED RASPBERRIES.

Let your raspberries be gathered on a dry day. Measure them, and to a quart of raspberries allow a pound of fine loaf-sugar. Spread the fruit on large dishes, but do not heap it; let every raspberry lie singly. Pound the sugar to powder, and sift it over the fruit.

Then have ready the same quantity of ripe currants. Squeeze them through a linen bag which has been wrung out of cold water. Prepare a pound of loaf-sugar for each pint of currant juice. Put the sugar into a preserving-kettle, and pour the currant-juice over it. When it has melted, set it on the fire, and boil and skim it for ten minutes. When no more scum rises, put in the raspberries. As soon as they are all scalded, take off the kettle, cover it, and set it away for two hours. Then put it again on the fire for about five minutes. Afterward set it again away for two hours, and then return it to the fire as before. This must be done three times in all, but on no account allow the raspberries to boil. If done with care, they will be whole and transparent.

When cold, put them up in glasses.

If you preserve white raspberries, do them in the juice of white currants.

Any other fruit may be done in jelly in the same manner.

ORANGE JELLY.

Peel twelve large sweet oranges, and cut them into small pieces. Put them into a linen bag, and squeeze out all the juice. Measure the juice, and if it does not amount to a pint, squeeze some more pieces of orange through the bag. Put a pound of double-refined loaf-sugar into a preserving kettle, and pour the juice over it. When the sugar has melted, put it over the fire. Dissolve two ounces of isinglass in a little hot water, and add it to the jelly just as it is beginning to boil. Let it boil hard twenty minutes. Then put it into glasses, and tie it up with brandy-paper.

Lemon-jelly may be made in this manner.

CLARIFIED SUGAR, FOR PRESERVES, AND OTHER USES.

To each pound of sugar allow half a pint of water, and half the white of an egg; thus four pounds of sugar will require a quart of water and the whites of two eggs. Mix the white of egg with the water, and beat it to a froth with rods. Take two thirds of the water, and pour it over the sugar. When it has melted, set it over the fire. When it rises and boils, pour in a little more of the water, and diminish the fire to abate the boiling and allow the scum to rise. Take it off, skim it well, and in five minutes set it on the fire again. When it boils a second time, add a little more water; and afterwards take it off and skim it again. Repeat this till it is quite clear, and no more scum rises. Then take it from the fire. Dip a fine napkin in warm water, wring it out, and then strain the syrup through it. Afterwards put your fruit into the syrup, and boil it till tender.

You may keep this syrup in bottles, and at any time you can put fruit into it; for instance, strawberries, raspberries plums, apricots &c. If only wanted for immediate use, you need not boil them, but send them to table in the syrup, with the advantage of their natural color and flavor.

FRUIT IN SUGAR COATS.

Prepare some of the best loaf-sugar powdered as fine as possible. Have ready some white of egg. Take some of the best and largest plums, cherries, strawberries, raspberries, apricots (peeled) or any other suitable fruit.

Dip the fruit, separately, in the white of egg, and then roll it all over in the powdered sugar, which will thus adhere to it, and form a coat. Then lay it on a dish (spreading it out so as not to touch) and set it in a cool oven to harden.

BURNT ALMONDS.

Take a pound of shelled sweet almonds, a pound of loaf-sugar, and half a pint of water. Melt the sugar in the water, and then set it over the fire. Put in the almonds, and stir them about till they are well dispersed through the sugar. Let them boil, and when you hear the almonds crack, they are sufficiently done. Take them off, and stir them till they are dry, and then put them into a wire sieve, and sift from them the loose sugar. Put this sugar again into the pan, with sufficient water to moisten it, and let it come to a boil. Then put in two spoonfuls of cochineal powder to color it red; add the almonds, and stir them over the fire till they are quite dry. Put them away in glass jars.

PEPPERMINT DROPS

Powder some fine loaf-sugar, add to it a little essence of peppermint (sufficient to give it a strong flavor) and enough of water to make it into a thick paste, which you must mix on a plate with the point of a broad knife. Then put the paste into a pan that has a lip or little spout at one side; melt it over the fire, and let it come to a boil. As soon as it boils, take it off and drop it from the lip of the pan into a clean broad tin pan or plate. Let the drops be all of the same size and shape. The tin pan that receives them must be very cold. As soon as the drops have hardened, loosen them from the tin, by slipping the point of a knife under each.

You may color them red with cochineal.

Keep them in a glass jar.

If the mixture congeals before all the drops are made, melt it again over the fire.

CHOCOLATE DROPS.

Scrape some of the best chocolate, and mix it with powdered white sugar. Moisten it with a little water, so as to make a paste. Work it on a plate with a knife. Then boil it in a pan with a lip, and pour it (a drop at a time) into a cold tin pan. While moist, sprinkle colored sugar-sand or non-pareils over the surface of each chocolate drop, which drop must be of a good shape, and about the size of a sixpence. When they are hardened, take them off the tin, by slipping under them the point of a knife.

Keep them in glass jars.

After the chocolate has boiled, make the drops as fast as possible; for if it gets cold before they are all done, it will injure it much to boil it over again.

The confectioners use for these purposes small leaden moulds, greased with oil of almonds. Into these moulds they pour the mixture, so that every thing comes out of the same size and shape.

NOUGAT.

This is a very fine confection. Take three quarters of a pound of shelled sweet almonds, and one quarter of a pound of shelled bitter almonds. Blanch them by scalding them in boiling water. Then throw them into cold water, and take them out and wipe them. Cut them into small pieces (but do not pound them,) and mix them well together.

Take a pound of loaf-sugar broken small, and mix it with half a pint of cold water, and an ounce of isinglass melted in a very little hot water. Boil the sugar, and skim it well. When it is quite clear, throw in your almonds, having first squeezed over them the juice of two lemons. Stir the almonds well through the sugar; and as soon as they are properly mixed with it, take the kettle off the fire.

Have ready a mould or a square tin pan well greased with sweet-oil. Put your mixture into it, a little at a time; dispersing the almonds equally through the sugar, before it has time to get cold. But if it does chill before the almonds are well mixed in it, set it again over the fire to melt. Turn it frequently in the mould, to prevent its sticking. When it has become a hard cake, set the mould for a moment in warm water, and turn out the nougat.

In stirring it, you had better use a wooden spoon.

ORGEAT PASTE.

Take half a pound of shelled bitter almonds, and a pound and a half of shelled sweet almonds. Blanch them, and pound them in a mortar one or two at a time, pouring in frequently a little rose-water, which will preserve their whiteness and prevent them from being oily and heavy. Pound them to a fine smooth paste, and then mix them with a pound and a half of loaf-sugar finely powdered.

Put the mixture again into the mortar, a little at a time, and pound it awhile that the sugar and almonds may be thoroughly incorporated; adding still a little rose-water.

When done, put it away in small covered pots or glasses, and it will keep several months in a cool dry place. It makes a very fine drink.

When you want to use it, put a small piece into a tumbler of cold water, and stir it till dissolved.

LIQUEURS.

To filter cordials, cover the bottom of a sieve with clean blotting paper. Pour the liquor into it (having set a vessel underneath to receive it), and let it drip through the paper and through the sieve. Renew the paper frequently, and fasten it down with pins.

This process is slow, but it makes the liquor beautifully clear.

NOYAU.

Take six ounces of peach kernels, and one ounce of bitter almonds. Break them slightly. Put them into a jug with three pints of white French brandy. Let them infuse three weeks; shaking the jug every day. Then drain the liquor from the kernels, and strain it through a linen bag. Melt three quarters of a pound of the best loaf-sugar in a pint of rose-water. Mix it with the liquor, and filter it through a sieve, the bottom of which is to be covered on the inside with blotting paper. Let the vessel which is placed underneath to receive the liquor be entirely white, that you may be the better enabled to judge of its clearness. If it is not clear the first time, repeat the filtering. Then bottle it for use.

RASPBERRY CORDIAL.

Take a quart of raspberry-juice, and half a pint of cherry-juice, the fruit having been squeezed in a linen bag after the cherries have been stoned. Mix the juices together, and dissolve in them two pounds of loaf-sugar. Then add two quarts of French brandy; put it into a jug, and let it rest five weeks. Afterwards strain it, and bottle it for use.

ROSE CORDIAL.

Take a pound of the leaves of full-blown red roses. Put them into a quart of lukewarm water, and let them infuse for two days, in a covered vessel. Then squeeze them through a linen bag, to press out all the liquid, and take as much white brandy as you have of the decoction of roses. To a pint of the infusion add half a pound of loaf-sugar, and a very small quantity of coriander and cinnamon. Put it into a jug, and let it set for two weeks. Then filter it through blotting paper, and put it into bottles.

QUINCE CORDIAL.

Pare your quinces, and scrape them to the core. Put all the scrapings into a tureen, and see that there are no seeds among them. Let the scrapings remain covered in the tureen for two days. Then put them into a linen bag, and squeeze out all the juice. Measure it, and mix it with an equal quantity of white brandy. To each pint of the mixture add half a pound of loaf-sugar, and a little cinnamon and cloves. Put it into a jug, and let it infuse for two months. Then filter it through blotting paper, and bottle it. This cordial improves by age, and is excellent.

LEMON CORDIAL.

PART THE EIGHTH.

MISCELLANEOUS RECEIPTS.

FRENCH COFFEE.

Let the coffee be roasted immediately before you want to use it, as it loses much of its strength by keeping. Its color, when done, should be a fine bright brown; but by no means allow it to scorch. A cylindrical coffee-roaster that can be turned by a handle, and sets before the fire, is far preferable to a pot or a pan. Grind the coffee while warm.

If you intend to make half a dozen cups of coffee for drinking, measure six cups of water of the same size, and put the water into the coffee-pot. Set it on hot coals, and when the water boils, put in two or three chips of isinglass, or the white of an egg. Then throw in six large tea-spoonfuls of ground coffee. Stir it several times while boiling, and set it several times back from the fire to diminish the boiling gradually. When it has boiled sufficiently, remove it entirely from the coals, pour in a cup of cold water, and then put it in a corner and let it settle for half an hour. Afterwards pour it off from the grounds into another pot (which must first be scalded), and set it close to the fire, but do not let it boil again.

If you intend to serve it up with hot cream, you must make the coffee stronger. While the coffee is clearing, boil your cream or milk, and pour some of it hot into each cup of coffee.

COFFEE WITHOUT BOILING.

Coffee made without boiling is much stronger, more economical, and less troublesome than the usual way; but it requires a pot of a particular construction. The best sort of pot for this purpose is called in French a Grecque (Greek). It must be made of the best block-tin, and of a tall cylindrical shape, with the spout very near the bottom. The receptacle for the coffee-powder fits into the upper part of the coffee-pot, and must be taken out when washed. The bottom of this receiver is pierced with very small holes, and there are two other strainers, made of movable plates of tin, also covered with fine holes. These two strainers fit into the receiver. The powdered coffee is to be placed between them, so that it may filter through the lower strainer, and also through the holes at the bottom of the receiver. Having scalded the pot, put the coffee into the receiver between the two movable strainers, and pour in some water which must be boiling hard at the time. The coffee will then drain through into the lower part of the pot where the spout is, and will clear itself in passing through the holes. Shut down the lid, place the pot near the fire, and the coffee will be ready for use as soon as it has done draining through.

Allow a large tea-spoonful of the powder for each cup that you intend to have.

This mode of preparing coffee is very expeditious, and requires neither isinglass nor white of egg.

CHOCOLATE.

Never boil chocolate in milk, as that spoils the flavor; and do not scrape it, but merely cut it into pieces. To an ounce of chocolate allow a cup of boiling water.

Having first scalded the pot, put in the chocolate, pour the water on it, and boil it till one third has evaporated. Then supply that third with cream or milk, and take it immediately from the fire.

You need not stir it more than two or three times.

FINE LEMONADE.

Allow a whole lemon and four or five lumps of loaf-sugar to half a pint of cold water. Roll the lemons hard on a table to make them more juicy. Cut them in half, and squeeze them over the sugar. Then pour on the water, and stir till the sugar is dissolved. Take out whatever seeds may have fallen in. In warm weather, put a lump of ice into each glass.

PUNCH.

Take three large lemons, and roll them very hard on the table to make them more juicy. Then pare them as thin as possible. Cut out the pulp, and throw away the seeds and the white part of the rind. Put the yellow rind and the pulp into a pint of boiling water; set it on the fire, and let it boil two or three minutes. Take it off, and throw in a tea-spoonful of raw green tea of the best sort, and let it infuse about five minutes. Then strain it through linen. Stir into it three quarters of a pound of loaf-sugar, and a pint of brandy, or any other suitable liquor. Set it again over the fire, and when it is just ready to boil, remove it, and pour it into a china bowl or pitcher.

CONVENIENT LEMONADE.

Take four ounces of powdered tartaric acid, and two drachms of essential oil of lemon. Mix them together, and keep them in a well-corked phial. A table-spoonful mixed with sugar and water, will make six or eight glasses of lemonade.

It will keep about a month, but not longer, as it will then lose its strength.

FRENCH MUSTARD.

Put on a plate an ounce of the very best mustard powder, with a salt-spoon of salt, a few leaves of tarragon, and a clove of garlic minced fine. Pour on by degrees sufficient vinegar to dilute it to the proper consistence (about a wine-glassful), and mix it well with a wooden spoon. Do not use it in less than twenty-four hours after it is mixed.

www.ingramcontent.com/pod-product-compliance
Lightning Source LLC
Chambersburg PA
CBHW081627100526
44590CB00021B/3636